MW01119737

Wen-Hsu Lin

General Strain Theory and Juvenile Delinquency

Wen-Hsu Lin

General Strain Theory and Juvenile Delinquency

A cross-cultural perspective

LAP LAMBERT Academic Publishing

Impressum / Imprint
Bibliografische Information der Deutschen Nationalbibliothek: Die Deutsche Nationalbibliothek verzeichnet diese Publikation in der Deutschen Nationalbibliografie; detaillierte bibliografische Daten sind im Internet über http://dnb.d-nb.de abrufbar.
Alle in diesem Buch genannten Marken und Produktnamen unterliegen warenzeichen-, marken- oder patentrechtlichem Schutz bzw. sind Warenzeichen oder eingetragene Warenzeichen der jeweiligen Inhaber. Die Wiedergabe von Marken, Produktnamen, Gebrauchsnamen, Handelsnamen, Warenbezeichnungen u.s.w. in diesem Werk berechtigt auch ohne besondere Kennzeichnung nicht zu der Annahme, dass solche Namen im Sinne der Warenzeichen- und Markenschutzgesetzgebung als frei zu betrachten wären und daher von jedermann benutzt werden dürften.

Bibliographic information published by the Deutsche Nationalbibliothek: The Deutsche Nationalbibliothek lists this publication in the Deutsche Nationalbibliografie; detailed bibliographic data are available in the Internet at http://dnb.d-nb.de.
Any brand names and product names mentioned in this book are subject to trademark, brand or patent protection and are trademarks or registered trademarks of their respective holders. The use of brand names, product names, common names, trade names, product descriptions etc. even without a particular marking in this works is in no way to be construed to mean that such names may be regarded as unrestricted in respect of trademark and brand protection legislation and could thus be used by anyone.

Coverbild / Cover image: www.ingimage.com

Verlag / Publisher:
LAP LAMBERT Academic Publishing
ist ein Imprint der / is a trademark of
AV Akademikerverlag GmbH & Co. KG
Heinrich-Böcking-Str. 6-8, 66121 Saarbrücken, Deutschland / Germany
Email: info@lap-publishing.com

Herstellung: siehe letzte Seite /
Printed at: see last page
ISBN: 978-3-659-29048-0

Zugl. / Approved by: University of South Florida

ACKOWLEDGEMENTS

I feel blessed by God who brought many people into my life to help and support my dissertation research. I thank my wife, Dr. Chen, for her dedication, without which I could not complete my goals. Of course, the gratitude should be extended to my parents who continually provide both financial and emotional support.

I acknowledge the hard work of senior researchers: Dr. Richard Dembo, Dr. Chris Sellers, Dr. John Cochran, and Dr. Thomas Mieczkowski. I thank Dr. Dembo, my dissertation committee chair, for helping me learn and adhere to a high standard of scholarship, and his support and mentorship throughout my graduate education.

I thank Dr. Sellers for enlightening me in theory and research, and for her extra guidance and help in exploring ideas that are reflected in this dissertation. I thank Dr. Cochran for his guidance and scholarly advice on my research practice. I thank Dr. Mieczkowski for encouraging me throughout my graduate education and agreeing to work with me. Each member contributed to my development as a scholar, and I would not have been able to complete this project without their individual effort and support. Special thanks should be given to Dr. James Schmeidler who sacrificially gave sound advice on guiding my statistical journey.

TABLE OF CONTENTS

LIST OF TABLES iv

LIST OF FIGURES vi

ABSTRACT vii

CHPATER I: INTRODUCTION.. 1
    Purpose of the present study 3
    Dissertation outline.. 5

CHAPTER II: STRAIN THEORY AS AN EXPLANATION OF
DELINQUENCY 6
    Review of classic strain theory 7
        Durkheim's anomie theory.. 7
        Merton's anomie theory 13
        Cohen's delinquent subculture theory.. 18
        Cloward and Ohlin's theory of differential opportunity and delinquent
            subculture 22
    Criticisms of the classical strain theory 26
    Modern strain theory and Agnew's general strain theory... 30
        Modern strain theory 30
        Agnew's general strain theory 32
            Strain 32
            Negative emotions.. 35
            Coping strategies 36
    Empirical assessment of general strain theory 38
        Strain-delinquency relationship 39
        The mediating effect of anger.. 42
    Agnew's revision of GST 44
    Empirical assessment of the revised GTS... 46
        Characteristics of strain and delinquency.. 46
        Other negative emotions... 48
        Summary and general limitations of previous studies 51

CHAPTER III: CULTURE, DELINQUENCY, AND GENERAL STRAIN THEORY............. 55
    Culture and its impact on the stress/strain process.. 56
        Dimensions of culture-individualism and collectivism..................................... 56
        Confucian ideology and its influence.. 62

The impact of culture on stress/strain 66
The impact of culture on negative emotions 70
The impact of culture on coping strategies... 72
Juvenile delinquency in Taiwan.. 75
Taiwan-an overview... 75
Juvenile law in Taiwan.. 76
Juvenile delinquency in Taiwan 77
GST in other non-western countries and Taiwan 87
Cross-national study.. 87
Applying GTS in non-western countries... 89
GST in Taiwan 93

CHAPTER IV: RESEARCH QUESTIONS... 97

CHPATER V: METHODS 99
Sample 99
U.S. sample 99
Taiwanese sample... 101
Survey preparation 106
Measurement of variables... 108
Delinquency.. 108
Physical aggression.. 110
Strain... 110
Failure to achieve positively valued goals-disjunction between
    Desired and actual outcome... 114
Failure to achieve positively valued goals-unjust outcomes............................. 114
Loss of positive stimuli-negative life-events 115
Presentation of noxious stimuli-victimization 115
Negative emotion.. 116
Demographic variables... 119
Analytic strategy 122
Statistical method... 122
Missing data 126

CHPATER VI: RESULTS 135
GST in the U.S... 136
GST in Taiwan... 148
Multiple group analysis 156

CHAPTER VII: CONCLUSION AND DISCUSSION 172
Summary of findings 173
Discussion of the findings.. 179
Strain and its characteristics 179
Negative emotions 183
Similarities and differences in GST across culture... 189
Limitations of the present study and future study 194

REFERENCES 198

APPENDICES 228
    Appendix A: Survey questionnaire 229
    Appendix B: EFA tables 231

LIST OF TABLES

TABLE 1   Juvenile Offender/Suspect Situation from 2004 to 2009 78

TABLE 2   Descriptive Statistics of Strain and Negative Emotion Variables.................... 120

TABLE 3   Frequency Distribution of Demographic Variables, Aggression, and Delinquency 121

TABLE 4   The Relationship between all Strain Variables, Delinquency and Aggression in the U.S. 139

TABLE 5   The Full GST Model in the U.S... 142

TABLE 6   The Indirect Effects of Strains on Outcome Variables through Anger and Depression in the U.S.. 145

TABLE 7   The Direct, Indirect, and Total Effects in the U.S. 147

TABLE 8   The Relationship between all Strain Variables, Delinquency and Aggression in Taiwan 149

TABLE 9   The Full GST Model in Taiwan.. 152

TABLE 10   The Indirect Effects of Strains on Outcome Variables through Anger and Depression in Taiwan.. 153

TABLE 11   The Direct, Indirect, and Total Effects in Taiwan 155

TABLE 12   The Full GST Model-Multiple Group Analysis for Delinquent Acts 158

TABLE 13   The Full GST Model-Multiple Group Analysis for Aggression....................... 159

TABLE 14   The Full GST Model-Multiple Group Analysis with Constrains (Damaging Property) 161

TABLE 15   The Full GST Model-Multiple Group Analysis with Constrains (Hitting Someone)... 162

TABLE 16   The Full GST Model-Multiple Group Analysis with Constrains (Alcohol Use) 166

TABLE 17   The Full GST Model-Multiple Group Analysis with Constrains (Aggression) 168

TABLE 18   The Wald test for Indirect Effect 170

TABLE 19   Summary for the Basic GST model in the U.S. and Taiwan 175

TABLE 20   Summary for the Full GST model in the U.S. and Taiwan 178

TABLE 21   Summary for the Indirect Effect of Anger and Depression in the U.S. and Taiwan 178

TABLE 22   Summary for the Tested Similarities and Differences in the Full GST Model between the U.S. and Taiwan 181

v

LIST OF FIGURES

FIGURE 1.   The GST Path Model 123

FIGURE 2.   The Iteration History Plot of Mean and Standard Deviation for the U.S.
             sample 133

FIGURE 3.   The Iteration History Plot of Mean and Standard Deviation for the
             Taiwanese sample 134

FIGURE 4.   The Path-Analytic Model of Strain and Negative emotions in
             the U.S. 141

FIGURE 5.   The Path-Analytic Model of Strain and Negative emotions in
             the Taiwan 150

ABSTRACT

General strain theory (GST) (Agnew, 1992, 2001, 2006a) is an established criminological theory. Although the theory has been examined by many and enjoys empirical support, some limitations of previous studies need to be addressed. First, previous studies have not incorporated all major types of strain in their models; hence, the effects of these strains on delinquency are unclear. Second, many previous studies did not include negative emotions and even negative emotions other than anger. Finally, and the most serious limitation, many previous studies rely heavily on samples from Western countries, mostly the U.S.; thus, possible cultural influences are ignored. Although a few studies have moved forward by using subjects from Asia (e.g., China, Korea), these studies only provide empirical results regarding whether GST is applicable in other cultures. The lack of comparable samples from both Western and Eastern cultures hinders direct comparison.

The present research contributes to the theoretical body of literature through addressing the aforementioned three limitations. First, the study measures the major types of strain that are mentioned by Agnew. Second, anger and depression are included in the analysis, which addresses not only the limitations of previous studies but also the suggestions of Agnew (2006a). In addition, the measure of anger is situational and consistent with GST. Thirdly, the present study uses the same research instrument to collect comparable samples from both the U.S. (Western country) and Taiwan (Eastern country). This enables a direct comparison across cultural boundaries, and the similarities and differences can be empirically established.

Whereas the core propositions of GST are supported, the study finds some negative results. In addition, most of the GST processes are found to be similar between the U.S. and Taiwanese juveniles. However, some differences were also discovered. Explanation of these similarities and differences from their cultural perspectives are offered. Furthermore, the results from this study also raise some challenges to GST and point out that revisions of GST may be required.

CHAPTER I:

INTRODUCTION

Psychologists and sociologists often refer to the period of adolescence as a time of storm and turmoil. One must understand that the connotation of "storm and turmoil" not only points out the high risks involved in various antisocial behaviors during this period (Goffredson & Hirschi, 1990; Moffitt, 1993), but also refers to the increasing stress and the levels of negative emotions that occur during puberty. Studies from the stress literature document that the juvenile period is fraught with struggles, distress, and negative emotions (Agnew, 1997; Compas & Wagner, 1991; Larson & Asmussen, 1991). Gore and Colten (1991, p.1) state "[T]he concept of stress is an important tool for organizing research seeking to understand development during the adolescent years." DuRant and colleagues (1995, p.233) also suggest that "[L]ife stress can have a deleterious impact on the psychological adjustment of adolescents," and the impact of such stress has been related to various negative outcomes including delinquency (Vaux & Ruggiero, 1983). Brandt (2006, p.58) concluded that "the increase and decrease in antisocial behavior are linked with increases and decreases in the levels of developmental stress associated with adolescence."

Studying the effects of stress or strain on delinquency during the adolescent years is important for two reasons. First, empirical studies have shown that there is a

1

relationship between strain and juvenile delinquency (Agnew, 2006a; Drapela, 2006; Seiffge-Krenke, 2000; Sigfusdottir, Farkas, & Silver, 2004). Second, delinquency not only causes immediate problems to juveniles (e.g., increasing victimization) (Kennedy & Baron, 1993) but also increases the risk of later life maladjustment (Moffitt, 1993; Sampson & Laub, 1993). In fact, scholars have found that delinquency during the adolescent years is a risk factor for later criminal involvement and negative life consequences (Elliot, 1994; Farrington, 1989; Nagin & Paternoster, 1991; Moffitt, 1993; Sampson & Laub, 1993; Tolan & Tomas, 1995).

Agnew's (1992, 2001, 2006a, 2006b) general strain theory (GST) is not only an important criminological theory (Cullen, Wright, & Blevins, 2006) but also used by many scholars to examine the strain/deviance relationship. This theory refines key concepts of classic strain theory (Cohen, 1955; Cloward & Ohlin, 1960; Merton, 1938), and provides a rich framework for analyzing the underlying mechanisms that connect strain, negative emotions, and delinquency in adolescents.

Although GST seems to be an important theory in explaining juvenile delinquency, some mixed empirical evidence suggests that GST can still be improved. Agnew (2001, 2006a, 2006b) revised GST from its original version in order to respond to this mixed evidence and criticisms. While examining the revised GST seems to be an important next step, without systematic examination of the basic and fundamental GST model seems premature and unwise.

2

Furthermore, extant tests of GST have relied almost exclusively on samples drawn from the U.S. Froggio (2007) raise a question regarding the utility of GST in explaining juvenile deviance in other countries. So far, only a few studies have applied GST in non-Western cultural settings (e.g., China, Korea, Philippine). Cultural attitudes and values influence one's definition of events and conditions as either typical or stressful (Chun, Moos, & Cronkite, 2005). Hence, a strain in the U.S. may not be seen as stressful in other cultures, which may not lead to subsequent negative emotions and delinquency. This raises some questions regarding the generality of GST. A single study that compares the similarities and differences in the GST process across nations is virtually non-existent (see Botchkovar, Tittle, & Antonaccio, 2009 for an exception). This is unfortunate because without comparative studies, both the generality of GST and its cross-cultural validity are questionable. Moreover, scholars have argued that cross-cultural studies could help to refine a theory so that such a theory is able to accommodate cultural differences (Kim, Triandis, Choi, & Yoon, 1994; Kohn, 1987). For example, Adler (1996) has argued that globalization offers a great opportunity to test and develop criminological theory. Moreover, Karstedt (2001) indicated that comparative studies "offer new insights, fresh theories and chances of innovative perspectives" (p.285).

Purpose of the present study

The present study addresses three gaps in the literature on GST. First, the present study will examine the effects of the three major types of strain on delinquency and negative emotions. Specifically, this study will measure the four different strains which cover all three major types of strain. Second, while most previous studies focus on anger,

3

the present study will include anger as well as other negative emotions, namely, depression as intervening variables in the strain-delinquency pathway. Moreover, the present study will examine the basic GST model by using a path analytic approach, which is useful in examining theoretically specified causal models and in exploring mediating effects.

Thirdly, most previous empirical studies use almost exclusively Western samples (e.g., American, Canadian). Only a few studies bring GST into Eastern cultural settings. A study that compares the GST process across Western and Eastern cultures is non-existent. The present study will fill this void by comparing the GST model as it operates in both the U.S. and Taiwan. This should either further establish the general scope of GST or demonstrate the need to further revise the theory to account for cross-cultural differences in strain, negative affect, and illegitimate coping mechanisms. Moreover, path analysis is able to implement multiple group analysis, a statistical method capable of comparing and contrasting theoretical models directly across different populations and providing statistically sound tests.

In sum, the present study is among the first that directly compares and contrasts the GST process between Western (U.S.) and Chinese cultures (Taiwan) by using comparable adolescent students from both the U.S. and Taiwan. In addition, the path analytic approach used to examine the basic GST model provides a new look at this model and provides stringent statistical tests on mediating effects (e.g., bootstrapping). This study includes adolescents from both the U.S. and Taiwan; hence, any similarities will not only support the core theoretical propositions of GST but also validate the GST model in both cultures. Moreover, any differences found could help to expand and revise GST to incorporate variation in cultures.

Dissertation outline

The dissertation comprises seven chapters in addition to the introduction. Chapter Two introduces the background and theoretical framework for classic and general strain theories. A thorough empirical review of GST will be included in Chapter Two. Chapter Three examines three related topics. First, the characteristics of culture in Taiwan and the impact of these cultural characteristics on strain/stress process will be reviewed, with a specific focus on how culture can affect strain, negative emotions, and coping behavior. Second, an overview of juvenile delinquency in Taiwan will be provided, which includes discussion of some specific delinquent acts in Taiwan that may vary from those in the U.S. due to environmental and cultural differences. Thirdly, a review of cross-national studies on GST and studies using a GST approach that are conducted in Taiwan will be discussed. Chapter Four gives a list of research questions that this study will address. Chapter Five describes the study's research design and analytic strategy. A specific discussion about cross-cultural research preparation will be given. Chapter Six describes the analytic results, and Chapter Seven presents a summary of findings, discussion of the findings, and limitations of the study.

CHAPTER II:

STRAIN THEORY AS AN EXPLANATION OF DELINQUENCY

Strain theory has a long history in both sociology and criminology. It can be traced back to Durkheim, although some have argued that Durkheim developed only a conceptual theme of crime, rather than a full anomie/strain theory of crime (Paternoster & Bachman, 2001). Nevertheless, Durkheim's analysis of the effects of anomie on suicide set the foundation for later development of anomie/strain theory. Decades later, Merton (1938) revised Durkheim's idea and proposed the influential anomie theory, which was intended to explain crime in America. Following Merton, Cohen (1955) and Cloward and Ohlin (1960) applied the concept of anomie/strain to subcultural delinquency (e.g., gang culture). Parsons (1951) also employed a similar idea of strain to explain individual deviant behavior and social control.

These leading scholars developed anomie/strain theory into a dominant paradigm in sociology and criminology. Although some scholars have argued that the classic anomie/strain theory is meant to explain only macro-level phenomena (e.g., social structure and crime rates) (Bernard, 1987), others have suggested that strain theory applies at the individual level and can be seen as an extension of Merton's anomie theory (Agnew, 1987). Regardless, the theory of anomie is best conceived as a macro theory (in

6

Merton's words (1964), "a sociological not an atomic theory"), and strain theory, which originated from anomie, is suitable for explaining individual level behavior (Paternoster & Bachman, 2001).

Although anomie and strain theories seem to have dominated empirical research in the 1960s, later critiques from other criminologists (Hirschi, 1969; Kornhauser, 1978; Bernard, 1984) have dampened its dominant status in criminology. Agnew (1992; 2001), in responding to the criticisms, outlined a revised strain theory, which he called general strain theory (GST). Importantly, Agnew (1992, 2001) expanded the scope of the sources of strain and delineated the underlying mechanism that leads strained individuals to crime and delinquency.

This chapter first provides a review of classic strain theory, beginning with its origins in Durkheim's macrosociological anomie theory. The contributions of three principal strain theorists-Merton, Cohen, and Cloward and Ohlin- will be discussed along with the extant empirical evidence and criticisms of the theory. After a review of this historical background, general strain theory will then be thoroughly explicated and its empirical evidence assessed.

Review of Classic Strain Theory

Durkheim's Anomie Theory

Durkheim ([1897] 2006) indicated that a human being has two needs: physical/organic needs and social needs. The former refers to material needs, such as food and shelter; the latter pertains to the desire to pursue status and love through

7

developing relationships with others or society in general. These intrinsic needs[1] are not bound by any limit because, according to Durkheim, humans have the ability of "reflection," which pushes desire to another level whenever the current desires are satiated. He further stated that "[The] more one has, the more one wants to have, the satisfaction one receives only serving to stimulate needs instead of fulfilling them" ([1897] 2006, p.271).

Furthermore, Durkheim argued that "if nothing comes from outside to restrict it [desire], it can only be a source of torment for itself" (([1897] 2006, p.270). Hence, for things to be otherwise, desires/needs must be controlled. For Durkheim, nothing inside the individual could possibly set the limit for ever-craving intrinsic desires, so the regulatory control must come from outside, which is society: "Only society …can play this moderating role, because it is the only moral power superior to the individual whose superiority the individual accepts" (Durkheim, [1897] 2006, p. 272). Therefore, society is the regulator of needs. And the relationship between societal regulation and individual needs varies across two types of societies: mechanical and organic.

A mechanical society is formed based on the resemblance of members and social groups in the society. The interdependence among members and groups is minimal and each individual or social group is self-sufficient (Durkheim, [1893] 1947). In this type of society, solidarity is achieved through the resemblance of members and the high overlap

---

[1] Although Durkheim ([1897] 2006) argued that the physical needs (basic biological drives) are automatically regulated by the organism, physical needs are, to some extent, insatiable. For example, it is true one cannot eat or drink over the physical limits, but one can always crave for better (e.g., delicacy, exquisite apparel).

of individual *conscience* and *conscience collective*. Consequently, social cohesion among members of society is no longer an individual but a collective phenomenon. Mechanical solidarity is only possible as long as individual *conscience* submerges into the collective conscience. Moreover, regulation of societal members stems from this strong and defined state of common consciousness (*repressive* sanction/penal law). Individuals who violate the common consciousness are punished severely because the law holds the essential meaning of society and, to some extent, threatens the existence of the society. The repressive sanctions reaffirm and revitalize the *conscience collective*.

In contrast, an organic society is formed by diversity, so interdependence is high. Social groups and members depend on each other in an organized system: "[We] seek in others what we lack in ourselves, and associations are formed wherever there is such a true exchange of service—in short, wherever there is a division of labor" (Jones, 1986, p. 27). Durkheim argued ([1893] 1986) that an organic society, due to cooperative relations, has a higher level of division of labor. In contrast to mechanical societies, (primitive), the social order or solidarity in organic societies (advanced) is achieved through both *conscience collective* and individual *conscience*:

> For the organic solidarity to emerge, the *conscience collective* must leave untouched a part of the individual *conscience* so that special functions …may be established there; and the more this region of the individual *conscience* is extended, the stronger is the cohesion which results from this particular kind of solidarity." (Jones, 1986, p. 34)

9

In organic solidarity, the main purpose of the law (*restitutive* sanction) is not to punish the law breaker but to restore relations between individuals, or contractual parties, and to achieve original states before the offense began. As Durkheim stated, the sanctions (law) in an organic society consisted "only of *the return of things as they were*, in the re-establishment of troubled relations to their normal state" ([1893] 1947, p. 69, emphasis in original).

According to Durkheim ([1893] 1947), social solidarity indicates that the society integrates all individuals or social groups into a single entity. The degree of social solidarity can be understood through two dimensions: integration and regulation. A well regulated and integrated society, hence, achieves solidarity. But a society that deviates from either dimension threatens the harmony of the division of labor[2]; therefore, the regulation of individual appetite is weakened.

Although Durkheim did not focus his theory on crime, he did apply his theory to one type of deviance: suicide. He argued that the phenomenon of suicide could not be explained away by causes that lie within the individual, but instead can be attributed to social factors ([1897] 2006). As mentioned earlier, Durkheim classified society based on two dimensions of social solidarity (integration and regulation). An abnormal society in which each dimension verges on the extreme has a higher rate of suicide. Accordingly, four different types of abnormal societies exist, and each is conducive to a unique kind of suicide. The first two types of abnormal societies are at two ends of the integration

---

[2] Only organic solidarity (division of labor) is discussed because each society, according to Durkheim, is at a developmental stage of a process toward division of labor.

continuum. On the one end, where society is tightly united and the individual is absorbed by the collective, individuals commit suicide for social purposes. For example, in some primitive societies elders kill themselves in order to reduce the burden on the tribe, and in mordent society, soldiers might end their lives for the honor of the society. On the other end of the integration continuum, where a society is disintegrated, the individual is detached from the society that both gives him meaning and satisfies his social needs: "[The] link that attaches him to society has itself been relaxed" (Durkheim, [1897] 2006, p. 231). Consequently, social members commit egoistic suicide for the individuals' purpose. The third type of society, one polar on the regulation dimension, is fatalistic suicide, which is a product of the over-regulated society[3].

However, an anomic society—and its suicidal acts—is most related to the strain paradigm. According to Durkheim ([1897], 2006), an anomic society refers to inadequate regulation or normlessness, which is the other extreme on the regulation continuum. This state is highly conducive to abnormal behavior such as suicide[4]. For example, during an economic crisis, the suicide rate increases because of the anomic situation that individuals encounter in the society. The norms that regulate individuals are no longer appropriate because society fails to teach individuals to reduce their needs. Therefore, individuals living under an economic crisis cannot meet their needs by using means that

---

[3] Durkheim only mentioned this type of suicide as the result of a "pitilessly blocked future" or "excessive physical or moral despotism." And he recognized its rarity and assigned little importance to fatalistic suicide in modern societies.

[4] While Durkheim only related anomie to suicide, contemporary scholars have employed his idea to explain other social problems, such as homicide (Pridemore, Chamlin, & Cochran, 2007) and economic crime (Cao, 2007).

they used during the normal economic situation, and this casts an individual into an uncomfortable state. Durkheim claimed that "[individuals] are not adjusted to this condition and the very prospect of it is intolerable to them" ([1897], 2006, p. 276). Economic prosperity also results in an anomic state because the regulation of needs is broken, which leads people to attempt to satisfy limitless appetites. This condition pushes individuals into an uncomfortable state since an individual constantly pursues unattained goals, which makes him or her feel unhappy. Therefore, whether prosperity or crisis, both situations lead to sudden social change, hence an anomic situation, which causes social problems.

In sum, Durkheim argued that sudden social changes, whether caused by crisis or prosperity, lead to the breakdown of social regulation, which in turn creates the state of anomie where the old rules of regulating are inappropriate and new rules are not yet formed. This anomic condition "unleashes escalating needs that outstrip means and ultimately pressure actors into committing suicide" (Cullen, 1984, p. 81).

Whereas Durkheim delineated the concept of the division of labor and various forms of abnormal societies and their relationship to suicide, Merton's anomie theory had more pronounced influence on later developments in strain theory. Merton (1938) revised Durkheim's anomie theory and constructed his own anomie theory, which was specifically developed to explain how inequality in the social structure and culture goals produced deviant adaptations in the United States.

Merton's Anomie Theory

In his "Social Structure and Anomie" (Merton, 1938), Merton revised the legacy of Durkheim's anomie theory and applied it to explain various deviant acts in America. Like Durkheim, Merton intended to develop a sociological explanation for deviant behavior in a society. Thus, he stated that "our primary aim lies in discovering how social structures *exert a definite pressure* upon certain persons in the society to engage in nonconformist rather than conformist conduct" (Merton, 1938, p. 672). Later in his writings, he proclaimed that "our perspective is sociological" (1968, p. 186).

Although Merton and Durkheim both attempt to use sociological theory to explain social problems, there are three major differences between them. First, Durkheim argued that deviance arises because of a breakdown in social regulation, which governs innate human impulse. In contrast, Merton stated that "the aberrant behavior may be regarded sociologically as a symptom of dissociation between culturally prescribed aspirations and socially structured avenues for realizing these aspirations" (1968, p.188.). Second, Durkheim referred to anomie as the failure of society to regulate or restrain goals and to provide suitable norms to follow (normlessness), whereas Merton referred to anomie as "a breakdown in the cultural structure, occurring particularly when there is an acute disjunction between cultural norms and goals and the socially structured capacities of members of the group to act in accord with them" (1968, p.216). Finally, Durkheim applied his theory only to one type of social deviance – suicide. Merton, on the other hand, is more ambitious in formulating a theory of different types of adaptations, which include various kinds of deviance (Cullen, 1984).

13

Merton (1938, 1959, 1964, 1968) conceptualized a social system as comprising two elements: a social structure and a cultural structure. The cultural structure can be defined as an "organized set of normative values governing behavior which is common to members of a designated society or group" and the social structure as the "organized set of social relationships in which members of the society or group are variously implicated" (Merton, 1968, p. 216). The cultural element was further divided into two subparts: the society's central goals or values (ends) and the institutionalized ways to achieve such goals (means). The "ends" referred to "culturally defined goals, purposes, and interests" that were "held out as legitimate objects for all or for diversely located members of the society" (Merton, 1959, p. 228); the "means" referred to a cultural structure that primarily defined, regulated, and controlled the normative modes of realizing culturally defined goals (Merton, 1959, 1968).

On the basis of these two concepts, the cultural structure (means and ends) and the social structure, Merton explained social systems in a systematic way. When there is equilibrium between the cultural structure and the social structure, that is, when the culturally approved goals could be realized by members of the collectivity via normatively prescribed means within social structural relationships, an organized collectivity or society is expected. In such an equilibrated society, where there is a harmonious relationship between the cultural structure and the social structure, individuals receive satisfaction both from achievement of goals and from striving to realize goals via institutionalized modes (Merton, 1968). Hence, success is twofold: "[I]t is reckoned in terms of the product and in terms of the activities." (Merton, 1959, p. 230).

14

The focus of Merton's theory, however, was to explain non-organized society (anomic society) based on his conceptions of the cultural structure (means and ends) and the social structure. A society becomes unstable because of a malintegration between the cultural structure and social structure and/or within the two elements of the cultural structure (cultural goals and institutional means). The former occurs when the culturally designated goals are universally applied but the access to the means is not equally distributed within the social structure. The latter refers to the situation in which the cultural goal is held at the highest position, while cultural means are relegated to a relatively low position. In such a situation, satisfaction is likely come to individuals who could not compete successfully either because access to the means is lacking or the means are inefficient. Merton stated clearly that "[I]f concern shifts exclusively to the outcome of competition, then those who perennially suffer defeat will, understandably enough, work for a change in the rules of the game" (1959, p. 230). Consequently, the technically most effective means that lead to achieving the moral mandate will be preferred whether it be "fair means" or "foul means" (Merton, 1968). Therefore, "as this process of attenuation continues, the society becomes unstable and there develops what Durkheim called 'anomie' or normlessness" (Merton, 1959, p. 231).

Based on the aforementioned conceptual scheme, Merton (1938) developed five types of adaptations to strain based on the discrepancy between cultural goals and institutional means to explain how an anomic social system induces deviant behavior. The first adaption, conformity, is the most common in a society; if this were not so, continuity and stability would not be possible for a society. Conformists are people who

15

not only accept cultural goals but also follow the institutional means to realize the goals. Because Merton's primary purpose was to explain deviant behavior, he did not spend much time on conformity.

The second type of adaptation, innovation, is of the most interest. This adaptation occurs when people internalize cultural goals but do not at the same time assimilate the institutional norms governing means to attain such goals. To Merton, this type of adaptation is the most common deviant adaptation and is closely related to crime (1968). Merton, then, employed this adaptation to explain the high crime rate among low SES groups in America. People in low social strata absorb the cultural goals, such as pecuniary success in America, but these individuals have little access to conventional means for achieving success due to either little education or limited economic resources or both. It is in these social strata that one can experience high levels of "innovation," namely, deviant behavior. Merton argued that "successful" innovative behavior lessens social norms, which intensifies the anomic situation for people in the system, and this, in turn, leads others to deviate in order to adapt to the severe anomic situation.

Ritualism, the third type of adaptation, is characterized by retention of institutional means but rejection of cultural goals. In Parsons' paradigm, this is seen in individuals who either passively conform to social or compulsively acquiesce to social norms (1951). For example, a government worker may realize that the opportunity of advancing in the social system is slim; hence, he or she may go to work and follow the rules just for the sake of "doing it." This kind of adaptation may not be highly deviant at first, but Merton argued that in the Western cultural model, "men are obligated to strive

16

actively…to move onward and upward in the social hierarchy" (1959, p. 246); therefore, departure from such expectations is deviant. Merton expected (1959, 1968) that innovation will be common in the lower class because of the prevailing emphasis largely on cultural goals with limited conventional opportunities or means. On the other hand, ritualistic adaptation should be heavily present in the lower-middle class because of successful socialization along with limited opportunities to climb the social ladder.

Retreatism, the fourth type of adaptation, is seen in individuals who abandon both cultural goals and institutional means. These individuals internalize both goals and means but constantly face conflict between ideology and reality; that is, the promise of success cannot be realized through conventional means. However, these individuals cannot adopt "innovative means" nor can they give up the goals or without renouncing the "supreme value of the success goal" (Merton, 1959, p. 250). To resolve this conflict, they abandon both the goals and the means. The escape is complete in that they are *in* the society but not *of* it.

Finally, the rebellion adaptation consists of creating new goals and means in addition to rejecting the original goals and means. Parsons described individuals who use this form of adaptation as actively alienated from the social system (1951). Merton argued that rebellion can be at two levels: the small and confined level and the endemic level. The former provides an opportunity for the genesis of a subgroup alienated from the community but unified within the group (Merton, 1959). Examples can be found in both Cohen's (1959) and Anderson's (1999) studies, in which cultural goals and means are replaced with "new" goals and means. The latter (endemic level) mainly refers to

17

large-scale rebellion that intends to substitute the goals and means of society at large, such as revolution.

In sum, Merton delineated the anomic society, within which the emphasis is greater on the cultural goals than on the cultural means and the distribution of institutional means to realize goals is unequal. In such a society, certain people will feel strain and frustration, which in turn lead them to respond in deviant ways. It is the explicit emphasis on structurally induced strain that make Merton's theory suitable for both macro-level (Bernard, 1987; Messner, 1988) and micro-level analyses (Agnew, 1985). However, Merton did not develop a clear explanation of the strain-delinquency relationship and ignored the presence of delinquent behavior in the subculture (Cohen, 1959). Merton also has been criticized for his neglect of the unequal distribution of different means to realize different ends (Cloward & Ohlin, 1960). Cohen (1955) and Cloward and Ohlin (1960) built on Merton's ideas to rectify these two limitations. The following sections will discuss first Cohen's theory and then Cloward and Ohlin's theory.

Cohen's Delinquent Subculture Theory

Cohen (1955) applied Merton's concept of anomie and strain along with societal interaction theory to explain the formation of the lower-class, male delinquent subculture. He argued that Merton's theory is valuable in explaining adult criminal acts or semi-professional juvenile thieves but is less valuable in explaining the lower status, male delinquent subculture. He also pointed out that Merton focuses on only one cultural goal-monetary success-and ignored another important goal-middle class status. In addition,

Cohen (1965, p. 9) criticized Merton for ignoring the anomic processes "whereby acts and complex structures of actions are built, elaborated, and transformed." In other words, Merton should have considered the process of interaction between several individuals, which may induce a deviant act (Clinard, 1964).

According to Cohen, all individuals are constantly involved in a series of efforts to solve problems, which are defined as "a certain tension, a disequilibrium and a challenge" (1955, p. 59). Problems come from two sources: the situation that one lives in and the reference frame that one employs. For Cohen, the most effective or satisfying solution to any problem must *"entail some change in that frame of reference itself"* (1955, p. 53, emphasis in original). The reference frame is variously defined by different subgroups, the most important of which are the "reference groups," which are more effective in defining the validity of the individual's beliefs and which are more powerful in providing incentives not to deviate from the established group norms (Cohen, 1955).

With the above conceptualizations, the core of Cohen's delinquent subculture theory is that lower SES males encounter a "status problem" or problem of adjustment in school. Cohen (1955, p. 65) argued that "status problems are problems of achieving respect in the eyes of one's fellows." Low SES males were not equipped with the middle-class standards or "middle-class measuring rods" (e.g., manners, nonaggressive behavior, studying hard) that teachers or school officials use to evaluate students. Students who study hard or behave well in class, for example, are more likely to gain "status" from the school system. The lower-status students, according to Cohen (1955), had not been educated in such ways in their social milieu. As a result, the "status" problem they

19

experience in school produces strain in these students, who were "beset by one of the most typical and yet distressing of human problems of adjustment" (Cohen, 1955, pp. 65-66).

Many lower SES students lack the characteristics or capabilities of gaining status in the larger society where they participate (e.g., school). One solution to status problems is for individuals who experience the same problems to congregate together and jointly establish a new standard of status that they could live up to. Accordingly, lower-class juveniles who experience a similar status strain interact with one another to find a solution to their common problem. After a long process of interaction (reaction-formation) and "joint elaboration of a new solution" (p. 60), these individuals come to form a new subculture, which Cohen argued earlier was the most effective and satisfying solution because it provides a new reference frame. This new reference frame, which entails "the kinds of conduct of which they are capable" (p. 66), satisfies the needs for "status" and thus reduces the strain. Although the subcultural solution to status strain is similar to Merton's "innovation" adaptation, or using "new" ways to achieve goals, the subcultural solution is a group solution, rather than a private one, because it defines status according to one's fellows and the criteria of the group.

According to Cohen (1955), there are many important characteristics of the delinquent subculture: "hedonism," "group autonomy," an orientation that is "malicious," "negativistic," or "non-utilitarian," and "versatility." Hedonism refers to little interest in long-term goals, planning activities or budgeting because the enjoyment of the here and now is the key. Group autonomy refers to intolerance of restraint, with the exception of

20

the informal pressure to follow group rules (e.g., loyalty). A malicious orientation refers to the enjoyment of the discomfiture of others and of defiance of social taboos (e.g., aggression). A negativistic orientation indicates the norms or standards in the delinquent subculture are antithetic to the norms of the larger society. Cohen (1955) argued that stealing is another way to achieve status, not merely an alternative means to acquire objects. Finally, Cohen observed that the delinquent culture is versatile, which negates the notion of "specialization." For Cohen, delinquents are involved in all kinds of "activities" in order to attain status. This concept of versatility is consistent with that of contemporary criminologists (Goffredson & Hirschi, 1990).

While the above paragraph describes how a delinquent subculture is formed, the methods of solving the problem of status frustration are not limited to the youths who interact together and form the delinquent subculture. Another solution can be found in youths who neither fully commit to the delinquent subculture nor repudiate all middle-class values. These youths, called "stable corner-boys," try to make the best of a situation through middle-class rules, but are also involved in some minor delinquent acts. Finally, the "college-boys" are those who endorse not only the middle-class goals but also middle-class rules. The differences between delinquent boys and college boys lie in the fact that the former repudiate both middle-class goals and rules and create a new set of rules to cope with the status strain, while the latter endeavor to achieve middle-class goals by following conventional rules. Finally, the stable corner-boys, although they commit delinquency, do not reject middle-class rules wholesale.

21

In sum, Cohen (1955) argued that lower-class adolescents lack the resources and social skills to succeed or gain status in school, where middle-class standards prevail, and this lack provokes status frustration or strain. The adolescents who share this same problem congregate together to create a new standard, that of the delinquent subculture, within which they can succeed and gain status. This new standard is in conflict with middle-class rules but provides a satisfying solution for these strained adolescents. Whereas Cohen focused on status strain in the lower-class group and the relationship between this strain and consequent delinquency and delinquent subculture formation, Merton paid attention to the goals-means discrepancy and its effect on different kinds of adaptation.

Cloward and Ohlin's theory of Different Opportunity and Delinquent Subculture

Cloward and Ohlin (1960) explored the formation of male delinquent subcultures in the lower social stratum, building on Merton's notion that the discrepancy between goals and means creates strain, which in turn, leads to delinquency. However, they argued that Merton ignored the fact that the distribution of illegitimate opportunities for success is not available to everyone. They also built on Cohen's concept that adjustment problems create strains for individuals, who then congregate together to find solutions, which introduces delinquent subcultures and delinquency.

Cloward and Ohlin (1960) argued that individuals in a society make an effort to meet or conform to social expectations or moral mandates and that such efforts "often entail profound strain and frustration" (p. 38). Furthermore, they stated that extending

22

socially approved goals under conditions in which conventional means are not available is the precondition for deviance and delinquency, as responses to strain or adjustment problems. To apply those basic themes to explain lower-class adolescent delinquency and formation of delinquent subcultures, they pointed out that the problems of such strains are disproportionally distributed in lower-class groups, are significant to these adolescents, and are permanent to these adolescents (1960). In addition, they recognized that there are barriers (structural and cultural) to reaching goals in this particular group, which makes the strain bear these characteristics and seem to be even more stressful. With these basic conceptualizations, Cloward and Ohlin continue by stating that lower-class youths who face such strains interact with one another in a long and complex process, which may provide "encouragement for the withdrawal of sentiment in support of the established system of norms" (1960, pp. 108-109). With the support of others who share the same problems, individuals may devise or adopt illegitimate means to achieve success. Also with such support, the anxiety and guilt associated with violating social norms is generally reduced, because allegiance to the conventional means is set aside, which in turn justifies the deviant means used.

While this group solution to a common adjustment problem is similar to the solution described in Cohen's (1955) theory, the point of departure lies in the outward attribution. Cloward and Ohlin (1960) argued that the formation of a delinquent subculture as a solution to an adjustment problem is likely only when individuals attribute their frustration to the unjust system rather than themselves. Lower class male adolescents face a relative discrepancy between institutional expectations and possible

23

means of living up to them because of the various barriers to achievement, which causes a feeling of discrimination; all these factors make the delinquent subculture solution, a group adaptation, highly likely.

Having delineated the source and process of forming the delinquent subculture, Cloward and Ohlin (1960) introduced another important concept: illegitimate means, which help to distinguish between three different delinquent subcultures: criminal, conflict, and retreatist subcultures. The means includes two things: the learning environment for acquiring required skills and values to perform a particular role, and the opportunity structure that enables individuals to fulfill the role (Cloward, 1959). A "[C]riminal subculture" develops in "integrated neighborhoods" where not only do conventional values and delinquent values coexist but also the different age levels of offenders are integrated well: "Unless the carriers of criminal and conventional roles are closely bonded, stable criminal roles cannot develop" (Cloward & Ohlin, 1960, p. 165). As the criminal roles are established, adult criminals provide role models for adolescents to emulate, and at the same time provide illegitimate opportunities to succeed. Consequently, the "criminal subculture" provides "means" for these adolescents to succeed, which in turn solves the problem of adjustment.

The "conflict subculture" develops in disorganized communities, which are unstable and transient. Such neighborhoods do not provide adolescents with legitimate means to succeed, nor do the communities provide criminal means to achieve goals. In addition, social control from both the conventional and the illegitimate sectors was loosened. Because both conventional and criminal means are blocked, adolescent

24

delinquents are left on their own to solve the adjustment problem. The only thing they can use to achieve "status" or "respect" is violent or physical conflict and, because of weakened social control, violence intensifies.

Finally, the "retreatist subculture" also emerges in disorganized communities. In addition to the same conditions as the previous two subcultures, youths who participate in this subculture lack both conventional and illegitimate means to success, whether criminal acts or conflict. Cloward and Ohlin (1960) called these adolescents "double failure." Because of the constant failure resulting from these restrictions, these youths escape from society in order to deal with their strain and frustration. Cloward and Ohlin (1960) argued that not all "double failures" youths adopt the retreatist subculture; youths might instead eventually become Cohen's "corner-boys," who live in accordance with the lower-class lifestyle. The difference is that retreatist adolescents are "incapable of revising their aspiration downward to correspond to reality" (p.184).

In sum, the theory of Cloward and Ohlin (1960) argued that lower-class male adolescents face adjustment problems or strains introduced by blocked legitimate means to realize cultural goals. In contrast to assumptions of previous theories, they pointed out that illegitimate opportunities are also not equally available to all adolescents who experience such strain. Consequently, those who become involved in the criminal subculture are those for whom illegitimate opportunities are available. For those who react with severe violent acts, both the conventional and the criminal means are closed but these adolescents possess physical ability or "guts." Finally, for those who lack all these means, the "double failure," the retreatist subculture becomes attractive. The major

25

contribution of Cloward and Ohlin (1960) was to introduce the opportunity structure into strain theory, to explicitly explain why some strained lower class adolescents become involved in one or another kind of delinquency.

Criticisms of the classic strain theory

This section will review some general criticisms of classic strain theory as a whole; however, some critiques of individual theorists will not be presented here[5]. There are three general criticisms of the classic strain theory (Cohen, 1955; Cloward & Ohlin, 1960; Merton, 1938): conceptual problems, limited empirical support, and limited scope of strain (e.g., focus only on goal-mean discrepancy) and delinquency (e.g., focus only on lower class delinquency). Strain theorists suggest that the imbalance of emphasis on goals over means in a society creates the pressure for its members to deviate; hence, it is the imbalance of culture that creates the motivation (strain) to commit aberrant behavior. Kornhauser (1978) argues that motivation to crime is not necessary because people naturally want more, as Durkheim would argue, and she also points out that the source of strain is due to "weak culture," not an imbalance of culture. The "weak culture" is the culture that fails to provide "public reorganization of moral worth" to its members who pursue their desired goals (Kornhauser, 1978, p.162). In her view, strain arises because a culture or a society does not recognize different goals that individuals in a society may pursue; hence, culture forces all members to live up to the same goal.

---

[5] For example, Kitsuse and Dietrick (1959) provided an excellent critique on Cohen's theory.

The second criticism, the lack of empirical support, is perhaps the most detrimental to classic strain theory. Most empirical studies operationalize strain as the discrepancy between aspiration/expectation of either high educational attainment or prestigious occupation. These studies usually do not find support for strain theory's prediction that those experiencing a large gap between aspirations and expectations would commit more delinquency/crime (Agnew, 1984; Akers & Cochran, 1985; Burton, 1991; Hirschi, 1969; Kornhauser, 1978; Elliott & Voss, 1974; Eve, 1978; Liska, 1971). Although most studies employing such an operationalization do not find support, Bernard (1984) contends that the more theoretically consistent measures of strain should be the discrepancy between aspiration/expectation of monetary success not the discrepancy between aspiration/expectation of educational attainment. Bernard suggests that education is only a means to meet the end; it is not the end in the classic theory. This argument is later supported by Farnworth and Leiber (1989), who argue that educational attainment is but one means to achieve economic success in the society. They find that the disjunction between economic goals and educational means predicts delinquency, especially serious utilitarian offenses. Similarly, Agnew and colleagues (1996) operationalized strain as dissatisfaction with monetary status, and they find that this variable strongly predicts income generated crime and drug use.

Although the common operationalization of strain is the discrepancy between aspiration/expectation of educational attainment or job satisfaction, other studies have focused on the blockage of opportunities to success. These studies usually measure strain as individuals' perception of their chances of achieving culturally approved goals. Burton

27

and Cullen (1992) argue that such a measure is more closely related to classic strain theory; however, the results from empirical studies are mixed (Burton & Cullen, 1992, pp.15-16).

Finally, classic strain theory focuses only on a limited type of goal (Agnew, 1985a), and its explanation of delinquent behavior is narrow (Akers, 2000). For Merton (1938, 1959, 1968) and Cloward and Ohlin (1960), the goal is monetary or material accumulation, and for Cohen (1955), the goal is middle–class status. Agnew (1985a) and others (Elliott & Voss, 1974; Elliott, Ageton, & Canter, 1979; Quicker, 1974) argue that youths pursue various goals (e.g., popularity, good academic performance) rather than limiting themselves to those goals that classic strain theorists have suggested (e.g., monetary success). In addition, the goals that adolescents recognize as important are not necessarily long-term goals; rather, they may be immediate goals, such as popularity in school.

Merton (1938, 1964) argues that the disjunction between goals and means in the lower class of a society creates strain, which motivates individuals to act deviantly (innovation). Cohen (1955) is interested in lower class adolescents who experience status frustration in school and respond through delinquency and the creation of a delinquent subculture. Cloward and Ohlin (1960) focus on strain, the lack of conventional and criminal opportunities to achieve a monetary goal, of lower class male adolescents and the consequent delinquent behaviors. All these theoretical arguments limit their scope in explaining lower class delinquency and delinquent subculture. As such, Agnew (1991) argues that the classic strain theory lacks the ability to explain the nature of middle class

28

crime. In addition, classic strain theory treats social class as a barrier that impedes individuals' achievement of culturally prescribed goals whereas Agnew (1991) suggests that other barriers might be at work (e.g., personality, skills).

In addition to the above criticisms, Agnew (1985a; 1991) argues that a related limitation of classic strain theory is that it focuses on strain that is introduced by blocking of the achievement of positively valued goals. However, another kind of strain, which is the blockage of escape from an aversive situation, is also an important cause of juvenile delinquency, because adolescents have relatively little power to change an aversive situation and they have not yet developed fully the mature cognitive and problem-solving skills and experience needed to cope successfully with these aversive situations (Agnew, 2003; DuRant et al., 1995). For example, whereas adults can move freely, within financial limitations, away from an aversive situation, juveniles are bound to their family and schools because they lack the means to move away (e.g., money, a car) and are legally compelled to remain in these situations. Steinberg and Cauffman (1996) suggest that psychological dispositions of the early adolescent (e.g., cognitive ability) lead many youths to make immature decisions about coping. Hence, two different kinds of strain can be identified; in the blockage of goal-seeking behavior, an individual is "moving *toward a valued goal*, but in the blockage of aversive avoidance, one is moving *away* from an *aversive situation*" (Agnew 1985a, p.154, emphasis in origin).

On the basis of these criticisms, Agnew (1985a, 1992), among other scholars, began to revise classic strain theory. First, the revised strain theory broadened the scope of strain to including strains from aversive situations and goals that were immediate to

29

individuals (e.g., good school grades). Second, the revised strain theory was able to account for delinquency in different social classes. This was in response to studies concerned with the results of self-report delinquency, which often revealed that juveniles from middle and high SES families also commit delinquent acts. Furthermore, the broadened scope of revised strain theory included strains other than economic strain, which were expected to be pervasive across SES levels. For example, students from different SES families all struggled with gaining autonomy from their parents. Consequently, parental control may be a common strain for youths. Third, the revised strain theory included social psychological dimensions such as negative emotions. The following section will briefly review "modern" strain theory (Agnew, 1991), and a detailed discussion of Agnew's general strain theory (1992) will then be given.

Modern strain theory and Agnew's general strain theory

Modern strain theory

The popularity of classic strain theory gradually waned in the 1970s because of the aforementioned limitations, especially the serious shortcomings of limited scope and lack of empirical evidence. Some scholars even suggested that this paradigm should be abandoned (Hirschi, 1969; Kornhauser, 1978). In responding to these criticisms, while still accepting the concept that failing to achieve desired goals through legitimate means produces strain and motivation to delinquency, modern strain theory focuses on three revisions: the characteristics of the desired goals, the barriers to realizing goals, and the cumulative effects of strain on delinquency (Agnew, 1985a, 1991).

30

First, modern strain theory proposes that the important desired goals of adolescents are not limited to economic success or middle-class status but include many other goals, such as good school grades or excellent athletic performance. In addition, modern strain theory contends that the goals of adolescents may be immediate goals (e.g., friendship) rather than long-term goals (e.g., occupational aspirations). Although studies indicate that adolescents pursue various goals and immediate goals (Agnew, 1984; Elliott & Voss, 1974; Quicker, 1974), results of empirical tests of these ideas have not been promising (Agnew, 1984).

Second, modern strain theory suggests that goal blockage increases the possibility of delinquency, especially when it causes the adolescent to fail to realize most of his or her goals. However, empirical tests of this proposition suffer from some limitations (e.g., measuring only some goal-blockage); they provide only mixed support (Agnew, 1984; Greenberg, 1979). Hence, Agnew (1985a, 1991) concludes that the revised modern strain theory, like its predecessor, receives only weak support. Furthermore, the various revisions that modern strain theorists have proposed attempt to accomplish only "patchwork" rather than providing a systematic explanation. For example, many of these revisions limited their scope of strain to the strain that classic strain theories conceptualized; that is, strain is induced because of failure to reach positively valued goals. These revisions, hence, focused on including different sources of strain (e.g., different goals) in response to the common criticism that aspiration/expectation discrepancy did not lead to, or was weakly related to, delinquency.

31

Agnew (1985a, 1992) took up the challenge and developed a more advanced and systematic explanation of the strain-delinquency relationship, which he labeled as general strain theory (GST). In contrast to all his predecessors, Agnew (1985a) introduced a different type of strain − failure to escape from aversive situations or stimuli. Furthermore, he included the concept of anger and conditioning factors, although the latter only implicitly. He found that individuals who could not escape from an aversive environment were more likely to be involved in delinquency, interpersonal aggression, and escape behavior directly and indirectly through anger; and the results were significant even after controlling for other theoretical variables (e.g., delinquent peers, attachment to mother). Agnew (1985a) concluded that this revised strain theory was able to explain middle-class delinquency and sporadic juvenile delinquency.

Agnew's general strain theory

After successfully introducing a new type of strain, "avoidance of aversive situations," Agnew (1992) further revised classic strain theory. He added another type of strain, provided a broader range of negative emotions, and introduced the concept of conditioning factors and coping strategies. This more systematic explanation of the strain-delinquency relationship was labeled general strain theory (GST). In GST, there are three central components: *strain, negative emotion, and coping strategies*.

<u>*Strain*</u>

The focus of GST is on negative relationships with others: "relationships in which the individual is not treated as he or she wants to be treated" (Agnew, 1992, p.48). GST

32

defines three types of major strains: (1) relationships in which others prevent the individuals from achieving positively valued goals, (2) relationships in which others present or threaten to present negative stimuli, or (3) relationships in which others remove or threaten to remove positively valued stimuli. The first type of negative relationship includes strains from classic strain theories (e.g., monetary strain) and strains from modern strain theory (e.g., doing well in athletics). The second type of negative relationship includes various situations in which the individual feels uncomfortable. Agnew (1985) pointed out that preventing individuals from escaping from an aversive situation does indeed increase the possibility of juvenile delinquency. The third type of negative relationship is commonly found in stressful life-events lists (e.g., death of family members).

Although the first type of strain was similar to classic strain theory, Agnew (1992, pp.51-53) further divided this type of strain (failure to achieve positively valued goals) into three subtypes: "the disjunction between aspirations and expectations/actual achievements", "the disjunction between expectation and actual achievements", and "the disjunction between just/fair outcomes and actual outcomes." The first subtype was consistent with classic strain theory, but Agnew did not limit himself to only monetary goals and included other immediate goals (e.g., popularity). He argued that the second subtype of strain, the discrepancy between one's expectations, which is more realistic, and actual achievements was more distressing. Compared with aspiration, which is idealistic and derived from one's cultural system, expectation is generated from one's "past experience and or/from comparison with referential or (generalized) others who are

33

similar to the individual" (Agnew, 1992, p.52). For example, classic strain theorists assume that a particular important aspiration for individuals in the United States is to achieve monetary success. In contrast, the expectation for an individual may be to achieve his or her parents' status. Hence, individuals who fail to achieve these more realistic goals might have stronger motivation to seek other means to achieve them. Finally, largely on the basis of the equity and justice literature, Agnew argued that individuals not only pursue goals, whether aspired or expected; they might also expect that fair or just rules will be followed in allocating rewards in each interaction. Consequently, when unfair or unjust outcomes are encountered, individuals might feel strain and have the desire to correct for such "injustice" so that they could gain more rewards, reduce their input, reduce others' rewards, or increase others' input. For example, one might steal something from the employer (gain a greater reward) or be uncooperative so as to increase the efforts that the employer must put into the job (increasing others' input) in an effort to reduce the strain resulting from an unjust promotion decision.

The second major type of strain refers to the presentation of negative stimuli. Negative stimuli can be social (e.g., discrimination) or non-social (e.g., natural disaster, illness). Individuals who experience such negative stimuli or aversive situations might become involved in delinquency in order to escape from the situation (e.g., skipping class), terminate or alleviate the negative stimuli (e.g., drug use), or seek revenge against the source (e.g., aggression).

34

The third type of strain derives from the removal of positively valued stimuli, which can be social (e.g., friendship) or non-social (e.g., materials). For example, the commonly used stressful-life event checklist in the stress literature usually includes items such as "loss of a boyfriend/girlfriend" or/and "death of a relative." Individuals who experience such strain might try to prevent the loss, to retrieve the lost stimuli, to obtain substitute stimuli, or to seek revenge against the source.

After describing the three major types of strain, Agnew (1992) specified the characteristics of strain that made it more influential. He suggested that strain that was of high magnitude, more recent, or of longer duration had stronger effects on consequent negative emotion and delinquency. He also argued that strains closely clustered in time had a particularly strong negative effect on individuals. For example, a bad score on one exam may not be so stressful but it becomes a strain when students not only get a bad grade but also have a fight with friends and lose a close relative. Although Agnew (1992) did not give more detailed descriptions of these characteristics, he later pays attention to these characteristics and elaborates upon them (Agnew, 2001).

Negative emotions

With three major types of strain having been delineated, GST explains the link between these potential strains and consequent delinquency. GST argues that each type of strain can lead the individual to experience an array of negative emotions, including anger, fear, and depression. Among the various negative emotions, anger is the most important to GST, because anger is very likely to increase an individual's level of

35

outward attribution of the injury, instigating the individual to act, motivating the individual to take revenge, and lowering the individual's inhibitions. Hence, anger influences individuals in various ways that are conducive to delinquency. Although anger is the most criminogenic emotion, delinquency might still occur in response to other negative emotions (e.g., depression). For example, anger might cause an individual to act aggressively against other individuals, whereas depression might lead the individual to take drugs in order to feel "better." Consequently, Agnew (1992, footnote 10) distinguished between outer-directed negative emotion (e.g., anger), which increases the likelihood of outer-directed actions (e.g., violence), and inner-directed negative emotions (e.g., depression), which lead an individual to show inner-directed responses (e.g., substance use). In sum, "[T]he experience of negative affect, especially anger, typically creates a desire to take corrective steps, with delinquency being one possible response" (Agnew, 1992, p.60).

Coping strategies

The third element of GST is the coping strategies that the strained individual uses to cope with strains and negative emotions. Agnew (1992) identified three major types of coping strategies: cognitive, emotional, and behavioral. The cognitive coping strategy mainly focuses on reinterpreting the strain in ways that minimize one's negative feelings. The individual can use this strategy in three ways to deal with the adversity. First, the individual can ignore/minimize the importance of the outcome. For example, one might say that "this is not important" or "money is not important compared with family." Second, one might maximize positive outcomes and minimize negative outcomes. For

36

example, Agnew (1985b) found that crime victims often stated that their victimization helped them to learn from it, which in turn reduced the negative feelings they attached to their victimization. Finally, individual might simply accept responsibility for the negative results so as to manipulate the input and output of themselves and others in a relationship. For example, one might claim that he or she did not work hard enough (minimize the positive input) or that others worked harder than they did (maximize others' input). As can be seen, this strategy is mainly a non-delinquent response.

The emotional coping strategies are responses that directly cope with the negative emotions resulting from a strain. Agnew (1992) offers several examples of emotional coping strategies, such as drug use, meditation, physical exercise, and various psychological techniques (e.g., playacting). Most of these strategies are conventional; however, drug use to reduce negative feelings could be antisocial (e.g., using an illegal substance).

Finally, there are three major subtypes of behavioral coping strategies: minimizing a negative outcome, maximizing a positive outcome, and taking vengeful behavior. To minimize a negative outcome, an individual can reduce negative feelings, terminate the cause of the negative outcome, or escape from the negative outcome. Several delinquent behaviors are explicitly related to such strategies; examples are substance use or skipping classes. To maximize a positive outcome, an individual can use means to increase his or her gain in a relationship or to retrieve valued goals. For instance, an individual may join a gang to gain support from gang members who will help the person to achieve goals (Cloward & Ohlin, 1960). Individuals may take vengeful behavior when they are strained in order to increase the inputs of others or decrease the positive outcomes for others. For example, adolescents might act incorrigibly to force parents and teachers to work harder to deal with them (increasing their inputs). Hence, behavioral coping strategies, rather than emotional or cognitive coping strategies, are closely related to delinquent acts.

In sum, Agnew's general strain theory (1992) advanced the classic strain paradigm in several ways. First, GST broadened the scope of classic strain (goal blockage) by including the discrepancy between expectations and real outcomes as well as unjust/unfair outcomes. The scope of strain was further expanded to include the presentation of noxious stimuli and loss of positive stimuli. Second, strain was seen as leading to not only consequent delinquency but also a myriad of negative emotions, which could also generate delinquency. Third, besides the cumulative effects of strain, other characteristics were incorporated into GST (duration, recency, and clustering). Overall, GST states that various strains can make an individual feel bad and want to do something about it, and whether the "something" is antisocial or conventional depends on various conditioning factors. GST provides a more comprehensive account of the strain–delinquency relationship than precedent strain theories. How this theory sustains empirical scrutiny will be presented in the next section.

Empirical assessment of general strain theory

Studies that test the various theoretical propositions of GST have thrived since its publication. While this body of literature is substantial, I focus on two empirical core

38

propositions of GST: (1) strains lead to consequent crime and delinquency, and (2) negative affect mediates the strain–delinquency relationship.

Strain-delinquency relationship

Most research on GST focuses on the relationship between various strains and consequent crime and delinquency. Early empirical tests conducted by Agnew (1985a, 1989) focused on presentation of noxious stimuli; he found a positive relationship between aversive family/school environments and various delinquent acts in a male adolescent sample. Agnew and White (1992) were the first research team to examine the strain–delinquency relationship in a systematic way. By using a large sample of adolescents (n = 1,380) from New Jersey, they found that various negative stimuli (e.g., negative life–events, neighborhood problems) had positive effects on delinquency and drug use, whether such relationships were tested longitudinally or cross-sectionally. Furthermore, this relationship remained significant even when rival theoretical variables were incorporated into the model (e.g., attachment, delinquent peers).

After Agnew and White's (1992) study, the inclusion of negative life-events became customary as a measure of negative stimuli, and the positive effects of negative life-events on delinquency and substance use were found in numerous subsequent studies (Aseltine & Gore, 2000; Aseltine, Gore, & Gordon, 2000; Broidy, 2001; Drapela, 2006; Eitle, 2002; Eitle & Turner, 2003; Hoffmann & Cerbone, 1999; Hoffmann & Miller, 1998; Hoffmann & Su, 1997, 1998; Mazerolle, 1998; Paternoster & Mazerolle, 1994). For example, Hoffmann and Cerbone (1999), using growth curve modeling, found that

39

experiencing a relatively high number of negative life-events over time was related to the "growth" of delinquency among adolescents, and these results could be extended to substance use (Hoffmann, Cerbone, & Su, 2000). Specifically, in adolescents who experienced increasingly stressful life-events over time, the reported frequency of delinquency and substance use also increased over time. In addition to negative life-events, researchers have used other variables to measure negative stimuli, including neighborhood/school problems (Johnson & Morries, 2008; Paternoster & Mazerolle, 1994), negative interpersonal relationships (Agnew & Brezina, 1997; Mazerolle, 1998), maltreatment or victimization (Baron, 2004; Brezina, 1998, 1999; Eitle & Turner, 2002; Harrell, 2007; Hay & Evans, 2006; Robbers, 2004), racial or gender discrimination (Eitle, 2002; Simons, Chen, Stewart, & Brody, 2003; Walls, Chapple, & Johnson, 2007), family strain (Hay, 2003), and homelessness (Baron, 2004, 2006; Baron & Hartnagel, 1997), and found these various negative stimuli were related to delinquency.

Studies have also investigated the relationship between failure to achieve goals and loss of positive stimuli. Robbers (2004; Baron & Hartnagel, 2002) found that goal blockage had effects on delinquency, and Ostrowsky & Messner (2005) found that traditional strain (failure to achieve positively valued goals) affected both property crime and violent crime. In contrast, Baron (2004) found that dissatisfaction about money was related to property crime but not to other types of crime (e.g., violent crime). Paternoster and Mazerolle (1994), who examined cross-sectional and longitudinal effects of traditional strain (limitation of goal attainment) on delinquency, found that traditional strain was related to delinquency in the cross-sectional model but only weakly or not significantly related to delinquency in the longitudinal model. Finally, Broidy (2001) used a college student sample to test GST and did not find support for direct effects of failure to achieve positively valued goals on certain measures of delinquency (e.g., property crime, drug use).

With regard to the effects of removal of positive stimuli and of composite strain, which combines various strains in a single measure, on delinquency, Mazerolle and Piquero (1998; Mazerolle, Piquero, & Capowich, 2003), using a sample of college students to test GST, found that removal of positive stimuli affected shoplifting whereas an unjust strain, in this case an unfair grade, led to fighting but not shoplifting; however, the effect of removal of positive stimuli became insignificant after controlling for other variables. The same research team also found that a composite measure of strain had direct effects on violence only (Mazerolle & Piquero, 1997; Mazerolle, Burton, Cullen, Evans, & Payne, 2000); in contrast, others found that a composite measure of strain affected different types of delinquent acts, such as property offenses (Piquero & Sealock, 2000), violence and substance use (Slocum, Simpson, & Smith, 2005).

In sum, a positive and significant relationship between strain and delinquency appears to exist. Specifically, the studies reviewed above have found that various stressors (e.g., negative life–event, unjust outcome, victimization) are positively related to various delinquent acts (e.g., violent behavior, substance use), and this positive relationship is found in both longitudinal and cross-sectional data. However, traditional strain (goal discrepancy) usually fails to stand out as an important predictor of delinquency.

41

Although these studies generally find supportive results, they reflect some limitations. First, not all of them examined all three major types of strain together. This could lead to possible model misspecification. That is, some important strains that are not included in the statistical model are treated as errors. Second, not all strains are related to all forms of delinquency. For example, Aseltine et al. (2000) found that family conflict directly affected juvenile marijuana use but not other forms of delinquency. Jensen (1995) pointed out that the definitions or types of strains are too broad and hence are unfalsifiable. Third, the magnitude of strain, such as severity or frequency of a strain, was not incorporated into these early studies. This is understandable, because despite Agnew's (1992) suggestion that the magnitude of a strain might make it more or less influential, he did not elaborate much on it. However, he (2001, 2006a, 2006b) later assigned great importance to these characteristics when he further revised GST.

The mediating effect of Anger

Another main proposition of GST is that strain not only has direct effects on delinquency, it also has indirect effects on delinquency through negative affect. By positing this, GST proposes that negative emotions will mediate the strain-delinquency relationship. Negative emotions in GST include various inner-directed negative emotions (e.g., depression, fear) and outer-directed negative emotions (e.g., anger), with anger as the emotional reaction most critical to GST. As a result, empirical research has focused almost exclusively on anger. Agnew (1985, 1989) found that aversive school and family environments had significant effects on anger, which in turn had significant effects on delinquency; and these results held up in both longitudinal and cross-sectional models.

42

Mazerolle and Piquero (1997, 1998) similarly concluded that strain had indirect effects on delinquency through anger. However, these studies and many others found that anger only partially mediated the strain-delinquency relationship; that is, strain affects delinquency both directly and indirectly through anger (Agnew, 1993; Agnew &White, 1992; Aseltine, et al., 2000; Hay, 2003; Hay & Evans, 2006; Mazerolle &Maahs, 2000; Perez, Jennings, & Gover, 2008; Sigfusdottir, Fakas, & Silver, 2004).

While the above studies found a partially mediating effect of anger, other studies have found fully mediating effects (Broidy, 2001; De Coster & Kort-Butler, 20006; Ford & Schroeder, 2009; Sharp, Brewster, Love, 2005). Broidy (2001) found that an unfair outcome was significantly related to anger, which in turn was related to crime. When both an unfair strain and anger were in the same model, only anger significantly predicted crime. Besides the issue of full or partial mediating effects of anger on the strain-delinquency relationship, studies also indicated some inconsistent results of the relationship between anger and delinquency. Some studies have found that anger does have effects on delinquency (Baron, 2004; Hay & Evans, 2006) whereas other studies only find that anger is only related to outer-directed delinquency (e.g., fighting) (Aseltine et al., 2000; Capowich et al., 2001). In contrast, Baron and Hartnagel (1997) did not find any relationship between anger and delinquency (e.g., drug use, violent and property crime) in their sample.

In sum, studies have usually found support for GST's mediating proposition that anger mediates the strain−delinquency relationship, whether the mediation is a partial or full mediating effect. However, some mixed results are also reported in the GST literature

43

that indicate that anger does not always have effects on delinquency or only has effects on certain kinds of delinquency. These results threaten GST's credibility because negative emotions constitute a central element of GST and one that distinguishes GST from other leading criminological theories. For example, family strain increases crime, which social control theory will argue is due to low attachment to parents. However, if the variable affects criminal involvement through negative emotions, such as anger, one can be more confident that the relationship between strain and delinquency follows GST's theoretical prediction.

Agnew's revision of GST

As reviewed above, two general limitations of GST can be summarized. First, although empirical evaluations generally support the strain–delinquency relationship, not all strains lead to all forms of delinquency (Mazerolle & Piquero, 1998; Broidy, 2001) resulting in a criticism that GST is "unfalsifiable" (Jensen, 1995). Furthermore, research has not specifically evaluated the effect of the characteristics of strain on delinquency. As studies from the stress literature suggest, the characteristics (e.g., magnitude, duration) affect which coping strategies one will use (Harnish, Aseltine, & Gore, 2000; Thoits, 1983). Second, empirical studies provide mixed support for the mediating effects of negative affect on the strain-delinquency relationship. Some studies find that anger is related to criminal acts (e.g., aggression, fighting) (Agnew, 1985; Baron, 2004; Hay & Evans, 2006) but not other kinds of delinquency (e.g., non-violent acts) (Baron & Hartinagel, 1997; Capowich et al., 2001), while others fail to find mediating effects of other negative emotions (e.g., distress, anxiety) on the strain-delinquency relationship

(Aseltine et al., 2000; Broidy, 2001). Furthermore, whether one should expect to find a total mediating or a partial mediating effect remains unclear. These limitations led Agnew (2001, 2006a) to revise GST further.

Revised general strain theory retains the central proposition of GST, which is that strain (the three major types of strain) leads to various negative emotions, which in turn affect crime and delinquency. However, the revised theory contains two major changes from this basic model. First, in regard to the problem with strain, Agnew (2001, 2006a) argues that strain will be most likely to cause crime if the strain is seen as: high in magnitude, unjust, associated with low social control, and creating an incentive for criminal coping. As such, forms of strain with these characteristics (e.g., abusive peer relations, negative school experiences, victimization) are regarding as criminogenic. For example, criminal victimization is one such strain (Agnew, 2001, 2006a, 2006b) because it is typically seen as unjust and high in magnitude, sometimes even traumatic (Kilpatrick, Sanunders, Veronen, Best, & Von, 1987). Moreover, criminal victimization, which usually occurs in peer groups where supervision is low or absent (Lauritsen, Sampson, & Laub, 1991), briefly presents a criminal behavior model (Agnew, 2006a). In contrast, strain that does not have these characteristics is less likely to cause delinquency.

Second, Agnew suggested that researchers should pay more attention to negative emotions such as depression and fear, which Agnew (2006a) suggests as key negative emotions, along with anger. Others echo such a suggestion (Capowich et al., 2001). Agnew argues that what GST proposes is state emotion, not trait emotion. The former refers to one's immediate experience of an emotion while undergoing strains. The latter

45

indicates one's propensity to experience a certain emotional states when facing strains (Agnew, 2006b). While this revision focuses on the role of negative affect in GST, Agnew (2006a) provides two other routes that explain how strain leads to delinquency. The first is that strains may temporarily reduce levels of social control, which in turn leads to delinquency. For example, negative parental treatment may temporarily reduce an adolescent's bond to the parents, and this reduced bond may increase the likelihood of delinquency. Second, strains may temporarily foster the social learning of crime that may increase the occurrence of crime. For example, criminal victimization may briefly expose individuals to a criminal model, which they might imitate. In summary, revised GST argues that strains lead to crime and delinquency through negative emotions, low social control, and criminal social learning of crime.

Empirical assessment of the revised GST

Characteristics of strain and delinquency

As the revised GST argues, some strains are more criminogenic than others, and such strains possess certain characteristics: high in magnitude, unjust, related to low social control, and association with criminal others and antisocial definitions. Empirical studies can be divided into two categories. First, studies that test certain criminogenic strains that were outlined by Agnew (2001; 2006a) generally found support. Specifically, strains such as victimization or vicarious victimization (Agnew, 2002; Baron, 2009; Hay & Evans, 2006; Harrell, 2007; Manasse & Ganem, 2009), discrimination (Eitle, 2002; Eitle & Turner, 2003), unjust/unfair outcome (Mazerolle, Piquero, & Capowich,

2003;Piquero & Sealock, 2004), parental rejection (Agnew, 2005; Hay, 2003), child abuse (Baron, 2004), homelessness (Baron, 2006, 2007), and a negative secondary school experience (Agnew, 2005; Moon, Hays, & Blurton, 2009) increased the likelihood of delinquency.

Second, there are only a handful of studies that directly test the effect of magnitude of strain on consequent delinquency. Slocum, Simpson, and Smith (2005) found that the best and most parsimonious model for explaining drug use included three dimensions of magnitude (duration, clustering, and accumulation); only two dimensions were significant in the model for violence (clustering and duration). They concluded that there appears to be some redundancy between the various dimensions of magnitude, and consequently researchers may not need to measure all of these dimensions in future studies. Other studies have focused mainly on the subjective evaluation of strain[6], which could be seen as measuring the severity of strain. For example, Froggio and Agnew (2007) found that adolescents from Italy committed more delinquent acts if they considered school failure and a romantic relationship breakup as more negative to them, compared to their peers who considered such strains as less negative. However, Botchkovar and colleagues (2009) found that severity of strain (subjective strain) did not improve the prediction of subsequent criminal responses among three European samples.

---

[6] However, Agnew (2006a) argued that researchers should distinguish between objective and subjective strain. The former refers to strains that are disliked by most people in a given group whereas the latter refers to strains that are seen as aversive by the people who experienced them. However, most measures of subjective strain asked individuals to indicate how big a problem (negativity) the strain was to them, which could be used to measure severity. Therefore, in the present study, subjective strain is regarded as severity of strain.

47

Other negative emotions

Only a few studies have investigated the effects of negative affect other than anger on delinquent adaptations (Broidy, 2001; Ford & Schroeder, 2009; Hollist, Hughes, & Schaible, 2009; Jang, 2007; Jang & Lyons, 2006; Kaufman, 2009; Sharp et al., 2005; Sharp, Terling-Watt, Atkins, Gilliam, & Sanders, 2001; Walls et al., 2007). Some of these studies have found that negative emotions other than anger increase deviant behavior. For example, Ford and Schroeder (2009) found that university students who experienced academic strain (disjunction between academic aspiration and actual outcome) reported higher levels of depression, and such students were more likely to engage in non-medical use of prescription stimulants. This particular study also found that depression fully mediated the strain-delinquency relationship. In another study, Sharp et al. (2005) found that negative emotions, combining depression, anxiety and guilt, mediated the effects of strain on eating disorders. Capowich, et al. (2001) found that negative emotions, such as feeling overwhelmed by life's demands, was related to shoplifting and DUI but not to fighting, and others found depression was related to substance use (Hoffmann & Su, 1998) and suicide (Walls et al., 2007). In contrast to studies that test the mediating effect of negative emotions, Brezina (1996) took a different view to testing the strain-negative emotion-delinquency proposition in GST. Specifically, GST argues that strains cause various negative emotions that in turn lead to delinquency, implicitly indicating that delinquency, as a coping strategy, would make the individual feel "better." Brezina (1996) found that strain did increase the level of negative emotions and that delinquency did help juveniles to reduce "bad" feelings.

48

In contrast, some studies have found null effects of negative emotions other than anger on delinquency (Aseltine et al., 2000; Hollist et al., 2009 Piquero & Sealock, 2000, 2004). For example, Piquero and Sealock (2000, 2004) reported that depression was not related to aggression and property crime, and Aseltine et al. (2000) found no support for a relationship between delinquency and anxiety and depression. Notwithstanding these mixed results, others who have examined the relationship between specific negative emotions and specific crime and delinquency, have suggested that inner-directed emotions (e.g., depression) affect inner-directed delinquency (e.g., drug use, social withdrawal) more strongly than outer-directed delinquency (e.g., aggression) (Jang, 2007; Jang & Lyons, 2006).

Another important issue related to negative affect is the different effects of trait-like and state–like emotions on delinquent coping (Capowich et al., 2001; Mazerolle et al., 2003). Trait–like emotion refers to one's tendency to experience a particular emotion across different situations, whereas state-like emotion refers to one's feelings in a specific situation. The majority of research has employed trait-like measures, which Agnew (2006b) argues as responsible for the mixed results of studies of mediating effects. Capowich et al. (2001), the first to measure the effect of situational anger on subsequent delinquent adaptations, found that situational anger fully mediated the effect of strain and other negative emotions (e.g., overwhelming feelings) on intention to fight. Mazerolle and colleagues (2003) further explored the issue of trait– and state–anger. They concluded that situational anger was strongly related to shoplifting and fighting whereas dispositional anger was related only to assault. They also suggested that anger

49

should be measured as situational, not dispositional. Ellwanger (2007) used a different method to measure state–like anger. He directly asked his subjects directly whether they felt frustrated or angry when a driving-related strain (e.g., traffic congestion) happened. He then combined strain with frustration and found this variable significantly affected driving delinquency.

Other studies that use more situational measures of negative affect other than anger have found some supporting results (Genem, 2008; Jang, 2007; Jang & Johnson, 2003). For example, Jang (2007) directly asked respondents what they feel when they experience strain, in order to measure state–emotion. He found that situational distress increased alcohol use as well as more conventional strategies of coping, such as religious coping. Genem (2008), using a scenario method, found that situational strain led to fear, which in turn increased the likelihood of cutting class. However, even with the scenario method, she did not find that situational depression predicted drug use. A recent study argued that because depression should be treated as a clinical disorder from the health perspective, distinguishing between state– and trait–depression is problematic (Manasse & Genem, 2009). This study suggested that depression measured by means of a clinical symptom checklist should be regarded as trait–depression. Consequently, the relationship between strain and trait-like depression is moderating rather than mediating (Manasse & Genem, 2009).

Summary and general limitations of previous studies

GST states that strains/stressors increase the likelihood of negative affect, that these negative emotions create pressure for correcting behavior, and that crime or delinquency is only one possible outcome. Whether an individual copes with strain and negative emotions in an antisocial fashion depends on several conditioning factors (Agnew, 2001a, 2001b, 2006a, 2006b). GST builds on this theoretical framework by describing three types of strain and four characteristics of criminogenic strain, negative emotions, and conditioning factors. It also delineates three mechanisms through which strain leads to delinquent acts. As reviewed above, empirical evaluation devoted to assessing GST is substantial. However, three general limitations in this body of literature require further investigation.

First, although previous studies have directly tested the effects of criminogenic strains on delinquency, more studies are needed, especially those that test the effect of unjust strains on delinquency. Equally important is that few studies have incorporated all the major strains in one model. Doing this may provide insights into how different strains affect delinquency simultaneously and the interrelationship between them.

Second, only a handful of studies have assessed the mediating effect of negative emotions other than anger, and the results are mixed. Some studies find support for the proposed negative emotions-delinquency relationship, but others do not. Still others find that negative emotions other than anger affect some types of delinquency, which indicates the possibility of a specific effect. In particular, inner-directed emotions (e.g.,

51

depression), affect only inner-directed behavior (e.g., substance use), whereas outer-directed emotions, mainly anger, influence only outer-directed delinquency (e.g., aggression). This specific effect has not been studied fully. In addition, whether state-emotion plays a mediating role whereas trait-emotion plays a moderating role remains to be verified. Furthermore, the theoretical importance of the new pathways through which strains lead to delinquency deserve more attention (Kaufman, 2009). Only two studies so far have directly examined these newly proposed mediating effects. Such limitations hinder further revision or refinement of the GST.

Finally, the most serious limitation is that most of the published studies have employed samples from the U.S. (Froggio, 2007), which hinders the generalizability of GST. Although generalizability could be explained as being able to account for various types of criminal acts, it also connotes the applicability of the theory in different societies or cultures. The GST process seems to be useful in explaining juvenile delinquency in the U.S., as reviewed above. Scholars have argued that researchers need to adapt and test the theory in other countries in order to increase generalizability and foster empirical development of the theory (Piquero & Sealock, 2000). In addition, Hoffmann et al. (2000) suggested that studies in other social settings are important for understanding fully the issues related to stressful experiences (Hoffmann & Su, 1998).

To complicate the matter further, many different cultures exist in the world (e.g., Chinese, Latino, African, European culture). So if GST finds support in the U.S., this may be replicated in other Western cultures, such as European countries (e.g., England) and Canada, because the general cultural settings are very similar. Indeed, Froggio and

Agnew (2007) found support for GST in Italy, and Baron (2004, 2006), who used Canadian street youth to test GST, also found similar results. However, Eastern cultures are different in several ways from Western culture. For example, Markus and Kitayama (1994) pointed out that in the United States, "it is the emotional states that have the individual's internal attributes (his or her needs, goals, desires or ability) as the primary referent that are most commonly manifest" (p.101). Hence, anger is often caused by other people who block or prevent individuals to achieve their goals. This assertion is consistent with strain theory. In a Chinese culture, which focuses on harmony within relationships and interdependence (Markus & Kitayama, 1991), negative emotions may be caused by failing to maintain relationships or meet others' expectations. The response to anger may also be different across cultures. For example, Tanzer and associates (1996) found that even secret criticism of others is considered a manifestation of anger in a Chinese culture because relationship harmony is so important; hence, even a subtle anger response should be controlled. In contrast, in America, expression of anger may be appropriate because it identifies individual needs and maintains identity (Markus & Kitayama, 1994). Therefore, the influence of culture on GST processes in Eastern cultures remains to be evaluated.

An even more valuable approach to addressing these limitations is to examine empirically the GST model in a cross-cultural study, within which an Eastern sample and a Western sample are included. By so doing, one can not only empirically evaluate the revised GST but also compare and contrast effects of cultural differences on these issues and on the GST process. As Kohn (1987) argued decades ago, cross-national studies provide an efficient method for testing, generating, and further developing sociological or criminological theories. The next section provides a review of culture and the differences between a Western culture (U.S.) and an Eastern culture (Taiwan). This review also provides an overview of crime and delinquency among adolescents in Taiwan. Finally, a section is devoted to review the empirical studies of GST in non-Western countries (e.g., Taiwan, China, Korea) and some cross-national studies.

CHAPTER III:

CULTURE, DELINQUENCY, AND GENERAL STRAIN THORY

Agnew's (1992, 2001, 2006a, 2006b) general strain theory (GST), which refined

key concepts of classic strain theory (Cohen, 1955; Cloward & Ohlin, 1960; Merton,

1938), has provided a rich framework for analyzing the underlying mechanisms that lead

strained adolescents to deviance. GST has been recognized by scholars as an important

criminological theory (Cullen et al., 2006) and has been used to examine the

strain/deviance relationship. However, it has relied heavily on studies in the U.S. and

other Western societies (e.g., Canada). This is unfortunate because, without comparative

studies, the generalizability of a theory and the validity of interpretations of the results,

based on research and theory from a single nation/culture, are questionable. Moreover,

even though some cross-national[7] studies have been completed, these studies are usually

still limited to the same "cultural frame" (Western culture). Cross-cultural studies have

shown many differences between Western cultures, mainly in the United States, Canada,

and some European countries (e.g., England, France), and Eastern cultures, mainly

Chinese culture (e.g., Taiwan, China, Singapore) (Hofstede, 2001; Triandis, 1995).

---

[7] Although the present study uses cross-culture and cross-nation interchangeably, one must always keep in mind that a nation can accommodate more than one culture (e.g., Native American cultures in the United States). The present study mainly considers the dominant culture in a nation as representative of that nation, such as Western culture in the United States and Chinese culture in Taiwan.

Consequently, to really test the generality of GST, one must test it across cultural boundaries.

The present chapter focuses on three topics. First, culture, the important dimensions of culture, and the differences between Western and Chinese culture are discussed in order to help define the concept of culture and identify the important cultural dimensions most responsible for cultural differences in the stress/strain process. Second, juvenile delinquency in Taiwan, which is used as the sample nation for Chinese culture, is discussed, focusing mostly on a description of juvenile delinquency trends and current situations in Taiwan. In addition, some aspects of the cultural and juvenile justice system background will be introduced. Finally, the current state of cross-cultural studies of GST, especially those conducted in Asia, and of studies that examine GST in Taiwan will be reviewed.

Culture and Its Impact on the Stress/Strain Process

Dimensions of culture–individualism and collectivism

Culture is one of the foundations of a society that affects the individual (e.g., how one views what strain is), as well as the environment (e.g., sources of strain). However, culture is both too broad and too abstract to be defined definitively. Kroeber and Kluckhohn (1952) concluded that a consensus definition of culture could not be attained after they had reviewed substantive literature and found 164 different definitions. Notwithstanding the abstract nature of culture, Lonner (1994) outlined several common ingredients in the definition of culture that can be summarized succinctly: (1) culture provides settings within which various human behaviors can occur; (2) culture creates the potential for individuals to react, and this potential changes over time and place, and (3) culture contains values, beliefs, attitudes, and languages that emerge as adaptation to the environment of a group of people (p. 234).Therefore, a definition of culture might be considered suitable if it contains these important components.

Chun, Moos, and Cronkite (2005, p. 31) stated that a "system [culture] of meaning encompasses the norms, beliefs, and values that provide prescriptions for behavior." Kroeber and Parsons (1958, p. 583) arrived at a similar and cross-disciplinary definition of culture as "transmitted and created content and patterns of values, ideas, and other symbolic-meaningful systems as factors in the shaping of human behavior and the artifacts produced through behavior" (see Laungani, 2004, pp. 15-23 for further review). In short, the present study will define culture to include shared norms, values, and beliefs that guide the behavior of members in a group; it serves to distinguish the members of one group from another (Hofstede, 2001) and plays a central role in affecting individuals' ideologies and behavior (Lam, 2007).

Among the many dimensions of culture, individualism and collectivism (Hofstede, 2001) have been recognized as important by scholars in various disciplines. For example, Parsons (1951), a sociologist, proposed the pattern variable of "self-orientation and collectivity-orientation." The former refers to the "pursuit of private interests" and the latter the "pursuit of the common interests of the collectivity" (p. 60). Hsu (1983), an anthropologist, not only recognized these two different dimensions of culture but also contended that the two ideas are primary and defining characteristics of the Western and

57

Eastern worlds. In addition to holding a similar view of individualism and collectivism, social and cross-cultural psychologists who have devoted a great deal of attention to this dimension and its impact on human behavior have introduced many concepts similar to individualism and collectivism, although these concepts relate more to the individual level than to the cultural level, such as Schwartz's (1990) concept of the contractual and communal society, Triandis' (1995) *idiocentic* and *allocentric*, Yang's (1986) individual-oriented and social-oriented self, and Markus and Kitayama's (1991) independent and interdependent self-construal.[8]

Although the definitions and connotations of individualism and collectivism are varied, common features of these two concepts can be incorporated in a consensus definition. Individualism refers to a society in which individuals are loosely linked and are expected to be independent and look after themselves. Such a society places a higher priority on self, and the individual is the central unit of society; consequently, self-fulfillment, emotional independence, individual rights, and autonomy are valued. Individualist societies emphasize "I" consciousness, and members give priority to personal goals over others' goals (Chun et al., 2006; Hofstede, 2001; Triandis, 1995). In sum, an individualistic society promotes the "independent self" (Markus & Kitayama, 1991), such that people place high value on independence, individual freedom, and personal achievement.

---

[8] Here, Triandis' idiocentric and allocentric, Yang's concepts of self, and Markus and Kitayama's self-construal are the presentation of individualism and collectivism at an individual level. All these different notations essentially deliver similar meanings. The present study will use individualism and collectivism, and these micro-level concepts interchangeably.

In contrast, collectivism, as a social pattern, refers to closely knit individuals and strong expectations of mutual support and loyalty. Collectivistic societies are oriented toward groups (e.g., family, nation), which are the central unit of society. Hence, obligation, interdependence, and fulfillment of social roles are the focal points. Collectivist societies stress a "we" mentality, and members are willing to give priority to the goals of the collective and emphasize group solidarity (Chun et al., 2006; Hofstede, 2001; Triandis, 1995). Collectivistic societies, then, cultivate an "interdependent self," such that individuals place a high value on cooperation, mutual support, and maintenance of group harmony.

The major difference between the culture of the United States and that of Chinese culture (Taiwan) is their different position on the continuum of individualism and collectivism. The United States, as an individualistic culture, can be documented in various historical accounts and other scholarly writing (Hsu, 1983; Bellah, Madsen, Sullivan, Swidler, & Tipton, 1996). For example, Tocqueville (1969) commented that America is a particularly "individualistic" culture (as quoted in Bellah et al., 1996). Similarly, Bellah et al. (1996) stated that "individualism lies at the very core of American culture" (p. 142). In contrast, Chinese culture has been described as a particularly collectivistic culture (Ho & Chiu, 1994; Leung & Bond, 1982). Hofstede (2001), the first researcher to systematically and empirically investigate the dimensions of culture internationally, analyzed over 116,000 questionnaires collected across 53 countries and identified four dimensions in which the cultures differed. Specifically, scores on individualism for the United States (91) were the highest among all 53 nations, whereas

59

Taiwan's score (17) was lower than the score of all but nine other countries. The scores for the United States and Taiwan also differed from each other for the three other dimensions: power distance, uncertainty avoidance, and masculinity vs. femininity[9]. In a nutshell, Taiwan, as a representative of Chinese culture, is more collectivist than the United States, according to Hofstede's empirical research.

Besides the above discussed differences between Taiwan and the United States on the individualism-collectivism continuum, the difference between these two countries is also manifested in various psychological concepts. For example, King (1981) maintained that an individual is treated as a psychological being in Western culture (United States), which is more individualistic, and as a social being in Chinese culture, which is primarily collectivistic. Similarly, Gabrenya and Wang (1983) found that Chinese from Taiwan and Hong Kong are more likely than their American counterparts to endorse group-oriented self-concepts. This particular result, along with others (Offer, Ostrov, Howard, & Atkinson, 1988; Triandis, 1989), reveals the difference in ideological self between Chinese and Western culture, which can be related to the cultural differences on the individualism-collectivism continuum. King and Bond (1985) concluded that the enduring prototype of the Chinese is the sense of belonging; in addition, Wilson (1970) pointed out that group loyalties and the idea of loyal behavior differentiated Chinese people from Westerners. In contrast, as Kim and Choi (1994) indicated, individuals in the United States were strongly encouraged to separate from their ascribed relationships

---

[9] In the present study, individualism versus collectivism is the focal point; however, there are three other dimensions of culture, based on Hofstede's study: power distance, uncertainty avoidance, and masculinity vs. femininity (the interested reader is referred to Hofstede, 2001).

(Bellah et al., 1996), such as family and relatives, and were encouraged to form other relationships based on common goals and interests (e.g., accumulation of wealth).

In addition to the aforementioned differences in the impact of individualism and collectivism, they also differ in their impact on how individuals interpret their "ultimate need," self-actualization (Maslow, 1943). For example, Yang and Lu (2005) listed three major differences between more individual-oriented and more social-oriented self-actualization. They argued that for individuals from Western cultures, particularly in the United States, self-actualization focuses on the internal-personal self; people want to enhance personal potential and characteristics that increase individuality and autonomy, and achieve personal rights and an egalitarian society. In contrast, for individuals from Eastern cultures, such as Taiwan, self-actualization emphasizes the social-relational self, self-cultivation, and self-improvement with regard to moral and personal skills, which lead people to realize their obligations in relationships in society.

In conclusion, since the concept of individualism and collectivism were derived, empirical research has thrived. The body of literature focuses largely on how individualism-collectivism impacts an individual's behavior cross-culturally. A systematic meta-analysis conducted by Oyserman, Coon, and Markus (2002) reached several conclusions regarding the influence of individualism and collectivism on an individual. First, although the U.S. is often singled out as more individualistic than most countries, such as African and Latin American countries, such a stereotype must be viewed with great caution. Second, Americans emerged as high in individualism and low in collectivism, and the differences between Americans and Chinese (e.g., Taiwanese)

61

were large. The authors further suggested that the difference between the U.S. and Chinese cultures on the individualism and collectivism continuum is more pronounced than the differences between other countries (e.g., African countries). Based on this discussion, this distinction is both theoretically and empirically sound. Nevertheless, although Taiwan and the U.S. may be meaningfully separated through individualism and collectivism, Confucianism ideologies, a salient cultural heritage unique to Chinese culture, are also important. The Confucian philosophy not only provides a deeper understanding of Chinese culture, but also provides a clearer view of the differences between the United States and Taiwan.

Confucian ideology and its influence

Confucian ideologies are closely related to collectivism and have been rooted in Chinese culture for centuries. The importance of the Confucian ideology in understanding Chinese culture in general, and Taiwanese culture in particular, can be found in several accounts. Bond and Hwang (1986) stated that center stage in almost all approaches to Chinese social behavior is occupied by the teachings of Confucius. Gallois et al. (1996) maintained that Confucianism provides the backdrop for the emergence of interpersonal relationships, self-concepts, and communication styles. Hofstede and Bond (2001) argued that the unique Eastern cultural dimension is Confucian dynamism. The present section deals with the significant impact of Confucianism on Chinese societies, a discussion that is suitably applied to Taiwan. Zhang (2003) argued that Taiwan is strongly influenced by the philosophy of Confucianism because most residents in Taiwan, regular citizens as well as those in government, are descendants of people from traditional Chinese culture.

The present review will focus on the immediate implication of the Confucian ethos for Chinese social behavior.

A fundamental Confucian assumption is that man exists in relationship to others and that harmony is the most treasured social value (Bond & Hwang, 1986; King & Bond, 1985). Moore (1967) further stated that in Confucian social theory, an individual is never conceived as an isolated unity; rather, he or she is treated as an interactive being. The proper way to maintain a relationship and to achieve harmony is prescribed by the dictate *li* (propriety), a set of rules on how to interact properly in daily life. The implication of *li* in daily life is exemplified in *wu-lun*, which delineate the proper interaction rules for five cardinal relationships—those between sovereign and subject, father and son, elder and younger brother, husband and wife, and friend and friend. Harmony is realized if each member in a dyad conscientiously follows the requirements of *li*. Consequently, Chinese people are commonly known to be peaceful and submissive, because of the emphasis on relational harmony, and each individual in a relationship is entitled to both rights and responsibilities. For example, parents receive their children's reverence and obedience; in return, they provide love and meet their children's needs. These relational rules echo Hofstede's (2001) results—Taiwan scored higher than the United States on "power distance." As relational harmony is conceived as cardinal, it is no wonder that a fundamental child-rearing practice among the Chinese, in general, is to teach youngsters to inhibit emotional expression of hostility toward others (e.g., authority figures) and, by extension, behavioral expression of aggression (Ho, 1986, 1996). This same confrontation-avoidance socialization pattern has also been observed by scholars in

63

Taiwan (Ho, Chen, & Kung, 2008; Yang, 1995). For example, Yang (1995) commented that the importance of relational harmony was instilled during early socialization, so that maintaining social harmony was deeply internalized in the individual.

An extension of the relational rule is the emphasis on filial piety (*Xiao*), which dictates intergenerational relations in the family. The family is considered the basic functional unit in the Chinese culture (Yang, 1995). The central meaning of filial piety for Chinese is to take care of parents, and on some occasions including senior extended family members. According to Taiwan Civic Law, it is the children's responsibility to support their parents, regardless of whether parents can support themselves.

To fulfill the mandate of filial piety, one not only takes care of parental needs, both economic and emotional, fulfilling obligations and showing an attitude of love and reverence, but also maintains the parents' "*mian zi*" (face), which means one should diligently pursue and maintain success in one's career–that is, success in the outside world (Lin & Liu, 1999)–to bring honor rather than disgrace to the family name (Ho, 1994; Lin & Lin, 1999). Another way to show filial piety is to submit oneself to parental wishes, especially the wishes of the father. Consequently, sacrificing one's own goals and replacing them with familial goals is not uncommon in Chinese society. As a result, Ho (1996) recognized that one of the characteristics of filial piety is acceptance of hierarchical ranking and authority.

Filial piety, as an important moral foundation of the family, also influences other interpersonal relationships. For example, certain significant social relationships, such as

64

master (teacher) and apprentice (student), operate on a simulated father-son basis (Lin & Liu, 1999). Hence, students show similar reverence and attention to masters or teachers as they would if the teachers were their biological parents. One famous Chinese saying summarized this mentality nicely: "yi ri wei shi zhong shen wei fu" (a teacher for one day, a father for one's entire life).

Finally, the focus on educational attainment affects individuals' daily behaviors and differentiates Chinese culture from Western culture. It is widely recognized that Chinese parents attach great value and importance to education and academic achievement (Ho, 1986; Sollenberger, 1968). Educational success allows one to pass civil service exams, which, in turn brings honor and glory to one's family, a fulfillment of the filial piety mandate. In addition, educational excellence allows one to climb the social ladder and achieve a successful political, social, vocational, and family life (Gates, 1987; Yang, 2004). Hence, educational attainment not only helps one to secure a share of the limited social resources but also fulfills the responsibility of filial piety, bringing the family *mian zi.* Shek and Lee (2007) found that Chinese parents place great emphasis on their children's academic performance, and believe that academic achievement is very important. Furthermore, parents are willing to invest greatly in their children's education and help them attain the highest education level possible (Ho, Chen, & Kung, 2008; Yi & Wu, 2004).

In sum, Confucian ideology affects Chinese society fundamentally, not only in the daily relationships regulated by his philosophy, but also in the extended aspects of

65

personal life, such as career decisions. The close relationship between the Confucian

ethos and collectivism is a factor in the cultural difference between Taiwan and the U.S.

The impact of culture on stress/strain

Because self-achievement, personal rights, and autonomy are the primary values

in an individualistic society, struggles in these areas in life may be stressful in that society

(Chun et al., 2006). In contrast, individuals from a collectivistic society, where relational

harmony and interdependence are more important, may see problems related to pleasing

parents and fulfilling family goals as more stressful. Compared to American college

students, Asian students (Hong Kong Chinese, Korean, and Japanese) have reported

higher needs for affiliation and more sensitivity to social rejection (Hui & Villareal, 1989;

Yagmaguchi, Kuhlman, & Sugimori, 1995). Heine and Lehman (1995) found that

Japanese college students, members of a collectivistic culture, considered interdependent

events (e.g., "Sometimes in the future you will do something that makes your family

ashamed of you") more stressful, and independent events (e.g., "After growing old, you

will find that you never realized your most important dreams") less stressful, compared

with Euro-Canadian college students.

In addition to the impact of culture on an individual's perceptions of stress/strain,

differences in parenting are pronounced between individualistic cultures and collectivistic

cultures. Whereas Chinese culture, as mentioned earlier, stresses obedience and proper

relationship rules, Western culture focus not on these matters, but rather on individual

rights and self-realization. Authoritarian (strict and controlling) parenting has been

66

determined to have a negative impact on school performance for U.S. children, but is related to a higher level of school performance for Chinese students (Steinberg, Dornbusch, & Brown, 1993). It is very likely that authoritarian parenting is considered illegitimate and unfair by American children but is perceived as showing love and concern by Chinese children. Hence, stern parental rules or discipline may be seen as a strain in the United States, whereas this same discipline may not be considered as a strain or at least be considered a less serious strain, in a more collectivistic culture or a culture with Confucian heritage, such as Taiwan. Consequently, coping behaviors in responses to such impacts may vary between these two countries, as found by Steinberg et al. (1993).

Differences between individualistic cultures and Chinese culture may also be found in interpersonal relationships. It should be clear by now that relational harmony is important in Chinese culture; as Yang (1995) pointed out, Chinese people are prone to an "other" orientation. That is, Chinese people worry about others' opinions, strongly conform to others, care deeply about social norms, and have a high regard for reputation. Students in the United States, especially graduate students, are encouraged to express their own ideas, criticize the ideas of others, and actively participate in class (Cross, 1990); hence, standing out is generally not regarded as stressful or undesirable. In contrast, Chinese students are often quiet and passive learners, and conforming to others is expected and desired (Yang, 1995). Hence, by extension, American students may not consider criticism from others as a strain that leads to negative emotions such as resentment, because it is a common practice. However, such criticism may cause strain

67

and consequent negative emotions in students from collectivistic cultures, such as Chinese students.

In addition, cultural differences have also been observed in influencing communication style. Empirical studies have shown that people from collectivistic cultures are more likely to use harmony-enhancing procedures—negotiating and complying—to deal with conflict processing; in contrast, individuals from more individualistic cultures are in favor of direct confrontation (Leung, Au, Fernandez-Dols, & Iwawaki, 1992; Leung, & Li, 1990). Although direct confrontation may make an interaction more stressful, it solves the problem more directly, making the strain relatively short lived. In contrast, harmony-enhancing procedures may reduce strain at the time of interaction, but they probably prolong the process and make the state of stress relatively long lived.

While cultural differences may result in different definitions of strain, they may also lead to similarities. In a collectivistic society, a verbal insult from an outside group member may be sanctioned, based on a "mind-your own business" rule (Bond, Wan, Leung, & Giacalone, 1985); hence, such an insult is likely to cause conflict and strain. A similar verbal insult in a more individualistic society invades personal identity, treasured in such societies, and these may also cause strain and conflict. Therefore, the same incident in different cultural settings may have the same results although the mechanisms or underlying meanings may be different.

While cultural differences affect individuals' perceptions and appraisals of the meaning/stressfulness of a particular incident, these differences also generate unique strains to the members of these cultures. As mentioned earlier, the Confucian heritage deeply influences Chinese society, especially the emphasis on education, which creates relatively high respect and high prestige for teachers at various levels of education. Therefore, examination-related strain and the harsh, sometimes seemingly abusive, discipline imposed by teachers is unique to students in Eastern cultures (e.g., Taiwan, Korea). These education-related strains and subsequent pathological states in juveniles have been documented in Korea (Morash & Moon, 2007; Moon, Blurton, & McCluskey, 2008), China (Bao, Haas, & Pi, 2007), and Taiwan (Li & Chiang, 2001; Xu & Hwang, 2004). For example, Li and Chiang (2001) reasoned that many juvenile delinquents may be "victims" of the educational system, which focuses too much on performance and ignores other important issues, such as the student's well-being.

Besides the above reviewed studies that provide direct evidence of the differences between individualistic and collectivist cultures, studies that obtained indirect evidence by evaluating the well-being of individuals have also helped to reveal cultural influences on strain. Oishi's (2003) cross-national study indicated that in more individualistic cultures, such as the United States, autonomy is emphasized; hence, the relationship between autonomy and life satisfaction is stronger in individualist nations than in collectivist nations. By extension, failure to fulfill the goal of autonomy leads to an unsatisfying life, which is stressful. To cope with such strain, according to GST, delinquency is more likely if autonomy has not been achieved (Agnew, 2006a).

The impact of culture on negative emotions

Emotional states and the expression of particular emotions are heavily influenced by culture. Although some scholars have identified a set of universal emotions (Ekman, 1999; Plutchik, 1980) and emotional responses (Mesquita & Frijda, 1992), the linguistic concept of an emotion, the antecedent of an emotion, and the expression of an emotion differ between cultures (Mesquita & Frijda, 1992; Russell & Yik, 1996). For example, in the Chinese culture, with its emphasis on social harmony and collectivism, expression of emotions, especially negative emotions, is prohibited or suppressed (Kleinman, 1986). Tanzer and colleagues (1996) found that anger responses are different between Singaporean Chinese women and their counterparts in Western societies. The expression of anger is prohibited or censured (Bond & Hwang, 1986) in Chinese culture; the maintenance of group harmony is so highly valued that even "secretly and quietly critiquing others" is considered anger expression.

Cultural influences with regard to negative emotions are not limited to expression of such negative emotions; they also affect how individuals feel in response to the same incident. In collectivistic cultures, communication is high-context and expressed implicitly; alternatively, communication is more direct and low-context in individualistic culture. As a result, training in the United States is more likely to focus on the speaker and speaking skills (e.g., how to deliver an idea clearly), and unskillful communication is likely to cause negative emotions (e.g., anxiety). Training in collectivistic cultures aims at the receiver or audience of the communication; misunderstanding on the part of the receiver leads to embarrassment or social criticism (Triantis, 1994, p. 185). Hence, the

70

same act, communication, may be a source of anxiety for the speaker in the United States, whereas in Chinese culture it is more likely to lead the perceiver to feel some stress and negative emotions.

As previously mentioned, authoritarian parental discipline may be considered a strain in the United States, but not in Taiwan; this difference in response to a parenting style may also cause different emotions in the two cultures. For example, one of GST's assertions (Agnew, 2006a) is that authoritarian (e.g., harsh) discipline leads to delinquency through increasing anger. In contrast, one in-depth study (Fung & Chen, 2001) found that Taiwanese parents explicitly and implicitly use shame to morally educate their children. By extension, this type of authoritarian discipline in Taiwanese culture will more likely increase the feeling of shame rather than anger, which may lead to a different kind of response. Therefore, while authoritarian parenting may very likely cause anger in the U.S., it is likely to elicit shame or other negative emotions in Taiwan.

From an independent-self perspective (Markus & Kitayama, 1991), self is more central, and expression and realization of internal and private attributes are the goals. For example, in the United States, emotional states that have the individual's internal attributes (e.g., one's needs) as the primary referent are more commonly manifested. The typical example from strain theories, both GST and classic strain theory, is that the blockage of goals is one cause of negative emotions, such as anger or frustration, and that expression of such negative emotion is not undesirable because it highlights the individual's needs and internal attributes and is consistent with the cultural framework (Markus & Kitayama, 1994). In contrast, in the cultural framework of Eastern Asia, the

71

goal is the alignment of one's reactions and actions with others (relational harmony). The most common negative emotions, such as anxiety, shame, or even depression are more likely to be related to relationships or a faltering of interdependence (Makus & Kitayama, 1994; Yang, 1995). For example, Yu (1996) argued that for the Chinese, failure to achieve a goal is usually blamed on the self, which is more likely to lead to negative emotions, such as anxiety, depression, or guilt.

The impact of culture on coping strategies

In addition to affecting the perception of stress/strain, consequent negative emotions, and expression of these negative emotions, culture is also related to how the individual copes with strain and negative emotions, because appropriate ways to cope and the resources one can draw upon, whether from others or oneself, are all culturally bound. The collectivistic culture and the Confucian heritage of Chinese society lead members of such societies to employ more interpersonal resources and fewer individual resources to cope with stress. In contrast, in more individualistic cultures, individuals are more likely to rely on the self. Indeed, Mu (1991) determined that Taiwanese adults are more likely than their U.S. counterparts to employ interpersonal social support to cope with stress.

The goal of coping may also be different in different cultural settings. Chun and colleagues (2005) suggested that in individualistic cultures, the primary goal of coping with conflict is to remove the barrier to a desired outcome, and to assert individuality and autonomy. In contrast, for an individual with a collectivistic orientation, the goal is to

72

manage conflict in such a way that no one is shamed and interdependence is reinforced and strengthened.

Individuals from individualistic cultures, compared to collectivistic cultures, have higher individual strengths or resources, such as an internal locus of control or self-esteem, and these in turn may lead to different coping strategies and outcomes. For example, alcoholic patients from the U.S. who use a behavioral approach to coping manifest lower severity of alcoholic problems (Chung, Langenbucher, Labouvie, Panadina, & Moos, 2001) because they believe that they are in control and trust their own abilities. These researchers also found that the patients who used fewer cognitive avoidance coping strategies had fewer interpersonal and alcohol related problems. In contrast, members of a collectivistic society are more likely to use avoidance strategies, although these coping strategies are not associated with maladaptive outcomes because of the belief that one is not in control (Chang, 2001; Yoshihama, 2002).

Self-esteem or mastery is usually called upon when one is under strain. As the GST and stress literature theorize, these personal characteristics can help to reduce the negative impact of strain on individuals' well-being (Agnew, 1992; Perlin, 1989). However, this may be true in predominantly individualistic cultures, where self is the focal concern, so that low self-esteem and a lack of the perception of control may increase the likelihood of maladaptation, such as crime. In more collectivistic cultures, self-esteem is different; some researchers (Lu & Yang, 2006) have argued that the self-esteem of Chinese people may be group self-esteem, so that the Western concept of self-esteem may not lead to positive coping behavior, whereas group-oriented self-esteem

73

may do so. Also, while a sense of control may be important, Confucian thinking emphasizes self-cultivation and virtue; therefore, low mastery may promote positive coping in the Chinese culture because it fosters perseverance.

Yu (1996) and Yang (1996) concluded that in Chinese society, success is usually attributed to others and failure to self, whereas the opposite was more likely among Westerners. Therefore, Chinese people are more likely to use self-directed coping strategies, such as self-improvement or self-blame; on the other hand, Westerners are more likely to use other-directed coping behaviors, such as escaping the situation or creating a new standard (Cohen, 1955; Cloward & Ohlin, 1960). For example, Heine and associates (2001) found that failing an experimental task is more likely to instigate Japanese students' corrective efforts for self-improving– that is, they tend to work harder on the same task. In contrast, Canadian college students are more likely to pay more attention to the experimental task at which they succeeded. The cause of the opposite result between these two cultures is that in a collective culture *mian zi*, or respect from others, is very hard to obtain; hence, instead of working to achieve something, students are motivated to work hard to improve their own shortcomings, so that their deficit will not jeopardize the *status quo* of their group or family.

In sum, although the cultural differences between the United States and Taiwan are many, they can be understood at least in part through individualism and collectivism, as well as Confucian ideology. Moreover, these differences manifest at each stage of the strain process. This section's discussion of the influences of culture on the strain process provides a systematic method of understanding the complicated relationships between

74

culture and the strain process. The next section will review juvenile delinquency in Taiwan and certain background aspects of Taiwan.

Juvenile Delinquency in Taiwan

Taiwan—an overview

Taiwan is located about 100 miles off the coast of southeastern China. Shaped like a yam, the island is about 247 miles long and 90 miles at the widest point and has a total area of about 14, 630 square miles. The total population is about 23 million. As of 2010, the population was largely composed of Chinese, numbering 23,162,123 (98%), and only 512,701 aborigines (Directorate-General of Budget, Accounting, and Statistics, Executive Yuan, R.O.C., 2011). Because of the population composition, Chinese culture is the dominant culture in Taiwan.

For the past five decades, Taiwan has experienced great economic progress. Major economic growth occurred in the 1970s, when annual rates of growth averaged 13.35%. It stabilized around 6.5% after the 1980s. The most significant change was the average annual per capita income, which was around $500 before 1970s but which rose to $16,432 during 2010 (Directorate-General of Budget, Accounting, and Statistics, Executive Yuan, R.O.C., 2011). In addition to rapid economic growth, Taiwan experienced political and social changes. For example, until the 1990s, when political liberalization occurred, Taiwan was under strict government control as a police/military state (Chu, 2000). During this long period of change, the family structure, considered the

75

foundation of Chinese culture, also underwent some changes. The double-income family with only one or two children is the main prototype in modern Taiwanese society.

Juvenile law in Taiwan

In Taiwan, juvenile delinquents include those who are between 12 and 17 and are subject to "Laws and Regulations Concerning the Management of Juvenile Matters" (*Juvenile Law*, 1981). *Juvenile Law* is intended to regulate not only delinquents, those who commit crimes, but also "potential offenders" (similar to "status offenders" in the United States), those who are situated in an environment where future offending is likely. Juvenile offenders are under the jurisdiction of the juvenile courts that operate at the local level, and the procedures are similar to those of adult courts, although juvenile trials are not open to the public (Chu, 2000).

According to the Juvenile Accident Act, two types of punishment can be given to juvenile offenders. The first type is mainly to "protect" youth, who are involved in minor offenses or who are considered "potential offenders": admonishment, weekend individual or group counseling, community service, protective or probation control measures, and reformatory school. Most judges are willing to sentence juveniles to these services/programs of punishment because the philosophy of the juvenile law is that it is better to teach juvenile delinquents rather than to punish them (Ho et al., 2008). This "teaching rather than punishing" mentality is consistent with Confucian philosophy. The second type of punishment, which is more serious and based on criminal law, includes imprisonment, fines, and detention. Juvenile offenders in Taiwan cannot be sentenced to

76

death or life imprisonment, unless the youth committed homicide of a lineal relative (e.g., biological parents or grandparents) (*Juvenile Law*, 1981). In addition to juvenile law, the Child and Youth Welfare Law, established and enforced in 2003, is designed not only to protect children (ages 0 to 11) and juveniles, but also to regulate and establish proper social welfare institutes. Such laws also emphasize parental responsibility for disciplining their children [10].

Within the current law enforcement structure, each police department has a juvenile corps unit, and specific projects or guidelines are established in city and county police departments, often known as the "Juvenile Guidance Section." The juvenile corps unit in each police department is responsible for both enforcing *Juvenile Law* and providing related services, such as referral to other resources and programs for enhancing parent-child relationships (*Introduction of Juvenile Guidance Sections*, 1991).

Juvenile delinquency in Taiwan

Juvenile delinquency became a serious problem in Taiwan during the period of rapid economic growth and social change, which included increased industrialization and change in family structure. Although juvenile delinquency has increased during this period (Chu, 2000, p. 211, Table 13.6), the number of juvenile offenders has decreased in recent years (Xu, 2005, p. 267, Table 1). Indeed, recent official crime statistics indicate that the total number of juvenile offenders/suspects was about 18,145 in 2003, but this

---

[10] For details about laws and regulations related to child and juvenile welfare, the reader is referred to Kuo and Wu (2003).

number decreased to around 11,283 in 2008 (National Police Agency, MOI, 2009) (see, Table 1). Compared with other countries, Taiwan's juvenile delinquency is very low. For example, juvenile offenders account for 9.9% of all criminal offenders in Taiwan in 2000; the figure is 37.4% for Japan and 17.1% for the United States (National Police Agency, MOI, 2002).

While recent official reports indicate that the number of juvenile delinquents is decreasing, the problem of juvenile delinquency has not disappeared. For example, a public poll conducted in Taiwan in 2002 revealed that the most worrisome serious crime problem is juvenile delinquency (27%). Another government report painted the same picture—Taiwanese citizens regarded juvenile problem/delinquency as a serious social problem (Research, Development, and Evaluation Commission, Executive Yuan, 2001).

Table 1 Juvenile Offender/Suspect Situation from 2004 to 2009

	Population of juveniles*	Juvenile offenders**	Juvenile delinquency rate (per 10,000)
2004	1,931,153	10,540	55
2005	1,948,681	9,620	49
2006	1,930,184	10,384	53
2007	1,944,062	10,881	56
2008	1,931,654	11,283	58
2009	1,936,831	10,762	55

*Juvenile population is based on age 12 to age 17 (Directorate-General of Budget, Accounting, and Statistics, Executive Yuan, R.O.C., 2011)
**Juvenile suspects/offender are between age 12 to age17 (National Police Agent, MOI, 2009).

A more academic survey showed a similar result in that "juvenile delinquency" was ranked among the top five most serious social problems during 1985-2001 (Taiwan Social Change Survey). The concern is not without empirical support. The early (1990s) studies revealed that juvenile delinquency was on the increase, reaching an unprecedented high in 1993 (Copper, 2003; Chen & Chen, 2000; Chu, 2000; Selya, 1995). And, as recent scholarly investigations have indicated, while juvenile delinquency seems to have decreased in recent years, the types of juvenile delinquency have changed. Chen and Chen (2000) argued that, although the number of juvenile delinquency suspects declined from 1990 to 2000, assaults and robberies more than doubled. Other scholars in Taiwan have also revealed that juvenile delinquency has become not only more violent, but also more prevalent (Hou, 2003; Kuo & Wu, 2003; Xu, 2005) than before.

Among juvenile delinquency acts, three are particularly serious and draw the most attention from scholars and the general public in Taiwan—violent crime, sex and Internet deviance, and substance use/abuse (Chen & Chen, 2000; Crime Investigation Bureau, 2008; Hou, 2003; Lee et al., 2009; Wu, 2001; Xu, 2005). Although total juvenile crime has decreased, the violent crime[11] rate increased from 15% of total crime in 1995 to 25% in 2004 (Xu, 2005, p. 269, Table 3). This increase in violent crime is mainly due to assault and an "offense against sexual autonomy" (Ministry of Justice, 2008; National Youth Commission, Executive Yuan, 2005). Two phenomena are related to these increases—joyriding and school bullying. In Taiwan, motorcycles are popular because of

---

[11] In Taiwan, a violent crime included assault, homicide, robbery, intimidation, and abduction. After 1999, "offense against sexual autonomy" was included.

their mobility, swiftness, convenience, and economy, which make them very suitable for traveling around dense cities and narrow streets. Almost every household has at least one motorcycle, which results in Taiwan having the highest number of motorcycles in Asia (Dai, 2005). Because motorcycles are easily available and fast, street motorcycle racing, which provides an exciting experience, is appealing. In many cases, juveniles who are involved in street motorcycle racing are in a small group (Xie, 1998), most of whom clams that the small group protects them and most of whom carry weapons (e.g., knives, bats).[12] As a result, violent attacks on rivals and even on innocent bystanders have become a serious social problem (Xie, 1998). For example, recently several joyriding juveniles randomly attacked and killed a young man in a park and similar incidents have commonly appeared in the news (see Xie, 1998, for a news review).

In addition, violence related to school bullying has increased and drawn attention in recent years. According to the Campus Security Report Center (2006), compared with previous years, in 2005, single assault incidents, which does not include group fighting, increased over 1.1 fold; other violence and delinquency increased about 1.3 fold, and intimidation and extortion increased over 2 fold. Another national self-report study revealed that 30% of junior-high school students (grades 7-9) reported they had been involved in some conflict with teachers or had fought with other students, and the figure is much higher, 50%, for senior-high school students (grades 10-12) (National Youth Commission, Executive Yuan, 2005). Other self-report studies have pointed out that large

---

[12] In Taiwan, firearms are illegal; hence, most criminals, adults or juveniles, usually carry knives and/or bats as major weapons. However, illegal gun ownership is also common among adult criminals, especially those in organized criminal groups or gangs.

numbers of students have either used violence against others or have been victims of violence on campus (Crime Investigation Bureau, 2008).

As mentioned earlier, the culture in Taiwan is highly influenced by the Confucian ethos, which emphasizes educational success and respect for teachers and other authority figures. Teachers and schools may be conferred a high level of authority to educate students, which sometimes involves physical punishment; this can easily lead to increased conflict between students and teachers. Moreover, as educational achievement is emphasized in Taiwan, students who do not do well in classes are usually marginalized in school, and many scholars argue that such marginalization is a major cause of school violence and other forms of delinquency (Hou, 2003; Lee, 1998; Xu, 2007). Moreover, as a result of the heavy focus on academic achievement, school curricula are mainly designed to reach such goals; hence, other activities less related to academics (e.g., physical education, music education) are relatively underdeveloped. This makes school education unattractive and sometimes burdensome, which could contribute further to an increase in campus violence and delinquency (Lee, 1998; Zhou, 2001).

Youth gang problems, which have become more serious in recent years, are also responsible for the increase in juvenile violent crime (Hou, 2003; Xu & Xu, 2000). Although youth gangs are not new in Taiwan, since the middle-1990s, they have become a social concern and a threat to many juveniles' safety. This problem is mainly due to adult criminal organizations extending their influence into schools by recruiting students from junior and senior high schools and marking their turf in these schools (Chai & Yang, 1999). A recent in-depth interview-based study indicated these gangs recruit students into

81

their groups because youth gang members are perceived to be "low cost," loyal, brave, and are likely to be given more lenient punishment by the law (Xu & Xu, 2000; Yang, 2004). Students who join gangs are looking for protection, friendship, and fun, and school drop-outs also consider gangs as a source of income (Xu & Xu, 2000). If youths join gangs mainly for protection, this implicitly indicates that gang members not only are seldom the target of criminal attacks, but also are "immune" from retaliation. Yang (2004) pointed out that the Confucian doctrines, which demand obedience and educational attainment, clash with the modernized (Westernized) social perspective, and this creates tensions between youth and social units (e.g., family, school). Students who struggle with these tensions are more likely to be rejected by family and school (school failure is commonly considered a shame to the family), so that often adolescents are left with few options but to join gangs that provide support and acceptance (Yang, 2004).

Taiwan has a high population density, and students typically have long school hours that include regular school hours (10 hours) and cram school hours (3 hours). Yi and Wu (2004) described students as highly stressed and strained. With insufficient outdoor recreational facilities, a result of Taiwan's high technology industries, and because of the influence of Japan, [13] several popular indoor entertainment businesses were born—cyber cafés and KTV. These two popular indoor leisure activities have been labeled as "crime-prone" places by society, and research has found that over 75% and

---

[13] Yi and Wu (2004) stated that Taiwanese youth admire the Japanese culture and this "involves both cultural dissemination and cultural assimilation" (p. 233).

54% of juvenile delinquents indicate they often go to cyber cafés and KTV, respectively, for fun (Zhou, 2003).

In cyber cafés, which provide high-speed Internet access and well-equipped computers, youth can enjoy online games and browse the Internet. According to a non-profit organization's national survey on youth, 51% of Taiwanese youth have been to a cyber cafe and 45% go to a cyber café once a week (Tosun Non-profit Organization, 2001). Because there are no adults monitoring how youths use the computers in cyber cafés, these cafés can become blind spots where adolescents congregate (students or drop-outs) and become involved in various deviant acts (Wu, 2001; Tosun Non-profit Organization, 2001). Although the most common activity is playing online games, over 25% of the survey respondents reported committing deviant or delinquent acts, such as prostitution, [14] browsing erotic websites, or buying pirated goods (e.g., CDs, DVDs).

Besides these types of online deviant behaviors, adolescents who linger in cyber cafés often become involved in related delinquencies, such as drug offenses. And, because of the anonymous nature of online dating and chatting, these activities provide a fantasyland for adolescents who are eager to make friends with opposite sex individuals, whose teachers and parents commonly believe that cross-sex friendships will have a negative effect on school performance. Moreover, because Taiwan is a collectivistic culture, communications between the genders and with strangers is more restrained than

---

[14] The problematic prostitution of young females is called Yuan-Zhu-Jiao-Ji in Chinese, which means young girls sell their body for material goods. The activity is believed to have originated in Japan. In the beginning, prostitution was arranged by phone, but now it mostly takes place through the Internet (e.g., instant message or discussion forum) and has become a "new social issue."

in individualistic cultures. As a consequence, many students become addicted to such non-realistic online activities, suffer harm (e.g., pregnancy), or become involved in risky behaviors, such as one-night stands, sexual promiscuity, or substance use (Huang, 2003; Wu, 2001). The high prevalence of Internet access, combined with the popularity of cyber cafés, has caused some scholars to point out that such a phenomenon partly accounts for increasing rates of "offenses against sex autonomy" as well as violation of copyrights (Xu, 2005).

Another popular indoor entertainment for Taiwanese youths is KTV (Karaoke TV) (Ho et al., 20008). It is similar to American karaoke, except that Taiwanese youth enjoy this activity in private rooms with friends. This type of entertainment is appealing, due to its privacy, which fits into the collectivistic culture of not standing out. Besides providing all the equipment, KTV facilities serve food and beverages. Hence, KTV has become a popular feature of gathering places for Taiwanese teenagers for various occasions (e.g., birthday parties) and entertainment. While KTV is enjoyable for many Taiwanese juveniles, it gradually has become a source of criminal and deviant activity. Due to its privacy and lack of monitoring, it is an ideal place for youth to engage in underage drinking and smoking, or even substance use/abuse and drug transactions (Yi & Wu, 2004). Several studies (Lee et al., 2009; Leung et al., 2008; Lee, Huang, Miao, 2000) have shown that KTV is one of the most common forms of entertainment linked to adolescents becoming involved in illegal substance use (e.g., MDMA, Ketamine). In some cases, deviant sexual behavior (e.g., date rapes) and prostitution are conducted in KTV establishments.

84

Finally, juvenile substance use and abuse[15] have become serious social problems (Ho et al., 2008), although junior and senior high school students who were convicted of violating substance regulation law numbered only 280 in 2007 (Zeng, 2008). However, that number represents 95% of the total student violators in Taiwan. Two official investigations also supported the belief that youth substance use and abuse are problematic. Compared with 2006, youth substance offenses increased 18% in 2007 (Ministry of Justice), and urine screen tests, completed by the Ministry of Education from 2006-2008, revealed that positive results for MDMA and Ketamine increased yearly from 231 (2006) to 420 (2008) (Department of statistics, Ministry of Education, 2008). Common substances used by the Taiwanese youth population are MDMA ("shaking head" pill), Ketamine, Amphetamine, FM2, and marijuana (Lee et al., 2009). Although the number of adolescents who use these illegal substances is increasing, the prevalence rate is still low, around 1% to 1.4% (Zhou, 2000). The increased use of these drugs, especially MDMA, is probably because it is cheap and provides excitement. High educational stress and the prevalence of some entertainment options (e.g., KTV) where adult control is low have been mentioned as causes of increased juvenile substance use and abuse.

In sum, although juvenile delinquency rates remain stable, this review points out that several important qualitative changes in juvenile delinquency have occurred in recent years. Consequently, the juvenile offending rate is still low in Taiwan, compared with the

[15] While this discusses only illegal substance use and abuse, alcohol and tobacco use are also common among students. For example, Ma (2000) found that 46% of the adolescents reported they had never smoked, and one culturally specific substance, the betel nut, is used by many adults, but its use is less common in the adolescent population.

rates in other Western countries, but it still draws societal attention. The traditional Chinese culture has gradually faded, due to economic growth as well as social and political changes. This cultural change has inevitably contributed to increases in juvenile delinquency. However, the traditional Chinese culture and Confucian philosophy have not been eradicated totally, and as a result the juvenile delinquency rate in Taiwan is lower than in most Western countries.

This review indicates that juvenile delinquency is somewhat different from that in United States because of specific cultural and social settings, such as the prevalence of motorcycles, cyber cafés, and KTV. This is consistent with Link (2008), who argued that juvenile delinquency depends on cultural attitudes and perception of the social structure and of differences in opportunity[16]. For example, because of the high population density and lack of land in Taiwan, juveniles engage in many different kinds of indoor entertainment, which encourages development of different kinds of delinquency than youths in the U.S. In addition, because of popularity of motorcycles, youths in Taiwan are involved in street racing and other kinds of delinquency (e.g., vandalizing properties) in which motorcycles, not cars, are used. However, although these studies and reports are informative, they are only descriptive and exploratory in nature. The next section will present studies that have employed GST to explain juvenile delinquency in Taiwan and in other non-Western countries, so as to provide a theoretical view of juvenile delinquency in these countries.

---

[16] One recent study on the victimization of drive-by street robbery also indicated that the uniqueness of this phenomenon is due to Taiwan's special social and cultural settings (Kuo, Cuvelier, & Chang, 2009).

GST in Other Non-Western Countries and Taiwan

The cultural differences between Western (United States) and non-Western countries (Taiwan) have already been discussed, and the possible effects of these differences on the strain process and juvenile delinquency have also been presented. However, studies that have examined GST in non-Western cultures are scarce. As mentioned in Chapter 2, the majority of the published studies are based on U.S. samples or samples from other Western countries (e.g., Canada). This hinders further development of GST and delinquency theory in general (Kohn, 1987). Kim and colleagues (1994) argued that cross-national studies would help revise a theory so as to better accommodate cross-cultural differences, and studies that directly apply GST in different nations have revealed the important role that culture plays in the GST/stress process (Bao, Haas, & Pi, 2007; Botchkovar et al., 2009; Chun et al., 2006; Markus & Kitayama, 1991; Tanzer et al., 1996). This section will briefly discuss the issues of cross-national studies and provide a detailed review of the few studies that apply GST in non-Western countries including Taiwan.

Cross-national study[17]

According to Kohn (1987), cross-national studies can be divided into different types according to their different purposes; two of these types are related to the present

---

[17] Although the present study uses cross-culture and cross-nation interchangeably, one must always keep in mind that a nation can accommodate more than one culture (e.g., Native American culture in the U.S.). The present study mainly considers the dominant culture in a nation as representative of that nation; hence, Western culture to U.S. and Chinese culture to Taiwan.

study. The first type consists of studies of particular countries or cultures for their own sakes. That is, the primary interest of the research is to know about, for example, Taiwan and the United States. By contrast, the second type of cross-cultural study focuses on how certain social construct/institutions influence individuals' behavior. In this perspective, culture is treated as the context within which theoretical mechanisms are examined. The present study intends to investigate the GST mechanism in two different countries, which leads to adoption of approach two. Consequently, the cultures in Taiwan and the United States are treated as the context that affects juveniles' perceptions of strain, the consequent emotional responses, and coping behavior. However, before comparing the GST process across nations, applying GST in Taiwan will provide insights into understanding the theoretical process in that country (approach one).

Despite the two types of research that Kohn (1987) defined, cross-cultural/cross-national research inevitably faces a related issue: the "*emic/etic*" issue. The former describes the study of a phenomenon within a particular culture ("*idiographic*" style). The latter tries to apply a general theoretical model to all cultures, in an effort to find universal behavior rules ("*nomothetic*" style). Using the *emic* approach helps ensure the uniqueness of a particular culture is preserved, but the generalizability of the results is limited, and there may be a risk of ethnocentricity. In contrast, applying the *etic* approach may greatly enhance finding law-like theories, but the approach risks ignoring cultural uniqueness. The present study, as a cross-national/cultural study, is a blend of *emic* and *etic* approaches because it transports and examines a theory that has developed mainly in the United States, within Taiwan, but at the same time the indigenous knowledge of

Taiwan is preserved because of the researcher's awareness. Also, the final results will be compared between the United States and Taiwan, which will help verify, revise, and extend the existing theory (Kim et al., 1994).

Applying GST in non-Western countries

So far, only six published studies have directly applied GST in three non-Western countries: China (Bao et al., 2007), South Korea (Moon & Morash, 2004; Moon, Blurton, & McCluskey, 2008; Moon, Morash, McCluskey, & Hwang, 2009; Morash & Moon, 2007), and the Philippines (Maxwell, 2001). In addition to these six studies, one other study investigated GST and crime across three Western European countries (Greece, Russia, and the Ukraine).

Maxwell (2001) used a convenience sample of sixth-grade students from one urban area of the Philippines to study the impact of family strain (witnessing domestic violence and parent-to-child violence) on antisocial behavior. Although the Philippino society is influenced both by Spanish culture (e.g., over 85% of the population is Catholic) and the culture of the United States (e.g., English is the medium of instruction), the Philippines are similar to many Eastern countries in that family is a significant social institution. The results of Maxwell's (2001) study indicate that witnessing domestic violence is a strong predicator of students' self-reported antisocial behavior and teachers' predictions about students' antisocial behavior. However, direct parent-to-child violence does not stand out as a significant cause of antisocial behavior. Maxwell argues that such null findings are consistent with Agnew (1992), and cautions against ignoring cultural difference in defining strain in cross-cultural research.

Bao, Haas, and Pi (2007), who applied GST in China, selected 615 students (grade 8 to grade 11) from Guangdong Province. They examined both the strain-delinquency relationship, as well as domain-specific and cross-domain buffering effects of several conditioning variables on this relationship. The results revealed that strain from family and school increases delinquency; however, negative relationships with peers do not increase delinquency. Regarding the domain-specific buffering effects, they found that school support dampens the effect of school strain on consequent delinquency. On the cross-domain buffering effects, they indicated that whereas family support reduces the effect of school strain on juvenile delinquency, school support protects youth from the negative effect of family strain. Finally, they found that moral beliefs buffer the effects of family, school, and peer strain on adolescents. This study also found that delinquent peers increase delinquency among students who experience family strain and school strain. The study also revealed gender differences in using social support. The authors argued that girls are more likely to use social support in managing interpersonal strain, but boys are more likely to be influenced by delinquent peers, which causes them to respond to interpersonal strain with a higher frequency of delinquency. School support plays an important role in modifying the strain-delinquency relationship in this study, which echoes the importance of Confucian influence in China.

Four other studies that use GST to explain juvenile delinquency in Eastern cultures were all conducted in South Korea. One study (Moon & Morash, 2004) recruited

385 11th graders from a large city in South Korea to examine the relationship between culture-specific strains (exam-related strain and teacher strain) and juvenile delinquency. This study revealed that teacher strain (emotional and physical abuse) did increase delinquency, whereas exam-related strain did not. In addition, teacher strain and delinquency relationships were conditioned by delinquent peer associations. The authors suggested that GST is applicable to South Korea but, at the same time, they advocated that researchers pay more attention to the specific types of strain unique to a particular culture. The same authors (Morash & Moon, 2007) also tested the gendered strain process that is delineated by GST (Broidy & Agnew, 1997). They found that boys are more likely to experience teacher strain and that, in both genders, the combination of teacher strain and delinquent peers is a strong predictor of violence. They also discovered that girls are under the influence of different sorts of strains—parental strain, teacher strain, and financial strain, than boys are. Girls who associated with delinquent peers were twice as likely to respond to these strains with delinquency than girls who did not associate with delinquent peers.

Unlike the two studies just mentioned, which investigated the basic GST process, two recent studies conducted in South Korea focused on claims of the newly revised GST (Agnew, 2001, 2006a). One of the studies (Moon, Blurton, & McCluskey, 2008) examined how the recent perceived injustice of key strains (e.g., criminal victimization) affect delinquency. Using a sample of 777 middle-school South Korean students, this study indicated that some key strains—teachers' punishment and criminal victimization—strongly predict juvenile delinquency regardless of whether such strains happened recently (in the past six months) or long ago (more than a year). This somewhat contradicts GST's prediction that says recent strain should have stronger effects on delinquency. Also, this study found that chronic parental punishment and bullying reduces delinquency. The perceived injustice of teachers' punishment and criminal victimization did not stand out as a significant predictor of delinquency in the full model, when other variables were included in the model (e.g., control variables). Furthermore, these authors revealed that anger increases delinquency, but does not have a significant mediating effect on the strain-delinquency relationship.

Using panel data based on South Korean middle-school students, Moon and associates (2009) conducted a "comprehensive" test of GST. They investigated the relationships between key strains, trait-based and situational-based anger and depression, several conditioning factors, and three different types of delinquency (violent, property, and status). In general, they reported that most of their strain measures, as well as a composite strain measure, had significant and positive effects on delinquency; however, bullying, as a strain, did not increase delinquency. This study also revealed that both situational and trait anger exert mediating effects on the strain-delinquency relationship, especially violent delinquency, but the influence of trait anger was only minimal. On the other hand, both trait and situational depression had slight mediating effects, even when inner-directed delinquency (e.g., smoking) was an outcome variable, which was inconsistent with GST's prediction as well as with results of previous research. Finally, Korean youths who experience various strains (combined strain) were less likely to commit violent crimes when they had a positive relationship with their parents, and such

92

adolescents were also less likely to become involved in property delinquency if they had higher problem-solving skills. Although this study reported that a strained juvenile was less likely to commit all forms of delinquency when this youth was associated with delinquent peers, these authors argued that such results might be artificial, in that within all levels of delinquent peer association, the strained students who had more delinquent peers were more likely to be involved in delinquency than strained students who did not, which was consistent with GST.

In sum, the above studies specifically applied GST to three Eastern countries and found support for some of GST's propositions, which supported GST's generalizability. However, as pointed out, some cultural influences were also apparent. For example, in Eastern countries, with their more collectivistic cultures, family plays an important role in youngsters' lives, which makes it a particular important source of strain. Also, since the Confucian ethos prevails in many Asian countries, teacher importance is emphasized. As Asian countries become more industrialized and modernized and, hence, more individualistic (Hofstede, 2001; Triandis, 1995), the conflicts between traditional role expectations and rules and modern individualized perceptions are expected to increase, which will inevitably increase feelings of strain.

GST in Taiwan

As Taiwan has experienced economic growth and has become more modern, juvenile delinquency as well as societal awareness of the well-being of adolescents have also increased. Hence, many recent studies have been conducted to investigate the effect

93

of stress on students and juvenile delinquency. For example, Li and Chiang (2001) reported that the most stressful life-events for youths (7th to 9th grades) are school-related incidents (Wang, 2001) and that students are more adaptive to stress when they receive material support (e.g., money, transportation). Xu and Huang (2004) also found that the most influential life stressor for Taiwanese juveniles is school stress and that such stressors are significantly related to various forms of delinquency, such as gang-related delinquency (e.g., joining a gang) and pirating (e.g., cheating, illegal copying). In contrast, Shi (2004) found that junior high school students who experience family-related, dating-related, peer-relational, or future-related stressors are more likely to experience higher levels of depression than those who experience school-related stressors.

Several studies have employed GST to explore the relationship between stress/strain and juvenile delinquency. Chen (2000) found that stress related to school is significantly correlated with delinquency and deviance; however, this stress significantly predicts only delinquency (e.g., stealing), but not deviance (e.g., cheating). Peng (2002) used a sample of junior- and senior-high school students from the southern part of Taiwan to investigate the relationships among strain, negative emotions, and juvenile delinquency. She found that negative life-events, daily hassles, and criminal victimization all have significant effects on delinquency; however, daily hassles fail to exert a significant effect on delinquency, when social control and self-control are in the model. In addition, criminal victimization and daily hassles cause negative emotions, and the combined negative emotions (e.g., anger, depression) along with victimization and daily hassles increases delinquency. Tsai (2005) and Xu (2005) both found that strain

94

significantly increases various delinquent acts (e.g., vandalism, gambling) and deviant acts (e.g., copying other students' homework) as well as some somatic symptoms (e.g., tiredness), after social support and demographic variables had been controlled for. Xu (2005) found that strain not only directly affects all these negative life-outcomes— delinquency, deviance, and somatic symptoms—but also indirectly affects them through negative emotions. [18] Tung (2007), who used a random sample of junior- high school students (n = 1,540) to investigate relationships between life stressors and violent behavior, found that negative life-events, relationship conflicts, and daily hassles all significantly increased violent behavior, even after controlling for social support, delinquent peers, and parental attitudes. In another report (Tung & Wu, 2008), the original three types of strain- blockage of achieving goals, presentation of negative stimuli, and removal of positive stimuli- was shown to be related to self-mutilation.

Although there have been a few studies that investigated the relationship between strain and juvenile delinquency in Taiwan, these studies have only scratched the surface. They focused on only the direct effects of various strains on delinquency, and only two studies examined the role that negative emotions play in the strain-delinquency relationship. Other important issues (e.g., conditioning effects) and the recently revised GST propositions (e.g., magnitude) have not been empirically evaluated in Taiwan.

In sum, while studies have employed the GST approach to explain juvenile delinquency in some non-Western countries (Maxwell, 2001; Morash & Moon, 2005;

---

[18] The author does not specify this variable except to name it as "negative emotion." Upon close reading, the items she uses to measure this variable are related to both anger and depression/anxiety.

Tung, 2003, 2007), these studies reflect certain limitations. First, studies applying GST to non-Western countries did not have a similar U.S. sample for comparison. Hence, the similarities and differences found in comparing the results to established evidence from the United States are subject to various explanations, including cultural differences, and sampling differences. Second, previous studies did not apply the full GST model, which includes all major types of strain and negative emotions, to other countries (see Moon et al., 2009, for an exception).

A more serious problem of many studies in the GST literature is the lack of a systematic explanation of cultural differences and similarities. For example, the most salient difference between Western (U.S.) and Chinese (Taiwan) cultures is the difference between individualism and collectivism, which are the concepts that scholars have identified as the major dimensions of cultural variability (Hofstede, 2001; Traiandis, 1995). How these two cultural variables interrelate with GST has not been explored. Also, how other important aspects of cultural heritage (e.g., the Confucian ethos for the Chinese) influence individuals' perception of strain, their emotional responses, and their choice of coping strategies has also been ignored. For example, Chinese culture emphasizes educational attainment and relational harmony, which may create or increase strains emanating from these areas in an adolescent's life. Furthermore, the expression of negative emotions will differ between Western cultures and the Chinese culture, because expressing negative emotions is a sign of immaturity in Chinese culture.

CHAPTER IV:

RESEARCH QUESTIONS

Drawing on the above discussion, there is a need to empirically evaluate the basic GST model and conduct a more systematic cross-national comparison, especially between Western countries and Eastern countries. This study uses a sample of U.S. adolescents and a sample of Taiwanese juveniles to address this gap in the literature. Specifically, the present study will address the following questions:

1. Is strain related positively to delinquency and aggression in the U.S. and Taiwan?
   a. Is goal strain related positively to delinquency and aggression in the U.S. and Taiwan?
   b. Is unjust strain related positively to delinquency and aggression in the U.S. and Taiwan?
   c. Are negative life-events related positively to delinquency and aggression in the U.S. and Taiwan?
   d. Is victimization related positively to delinquency and aggression in the U.S. and Taiwan?
2. Is strain related positively to anger and depression in the U.S. and Taiwan?
   a. Is goal strain related positively to anger and depression?
   b. Is unjust strain related positively to anger and depression?
   c. Are negative life-events related positively to anger and depression?

d. Is victimization related positively to anger and depression?

3. Does anger mediate the relationship between strain and delinquency/aggression?

4. Does depression mediate the relationship between strain and delinquency/aggression?

5. Is there any difference in the GST process in the U.S. and Taiwan?

    a. Is the strain → delinquency process different in the U.S. and Taiwan?

    b. Is the strain → aggression process different in the U.S. and Taiwan?

    c. Is the strain → anger process different in the U.S. and Taiwan?

    d. Is the strain → depression process different in the U.S. and Taiwan?

6. Is the GST mediating process different in the U.S. and Taiwan?

    a. Is the strain → anger → delinquency process different in the U.S. and Taiwan?

    b. Is the strain → depression → delinquency process different in the U.S. and Taiwan?

    c. Is the strain → anger → aggression process different in the U.S. and Taiwan?

    d. Is the strain → depression → aggression process different in the U.S. and Taiwan?

CHAPTER V:

METHODS

Sample

    This study includes two samples: one from the U.S. and the other from Taiwan. The U.S. sample is from an existing cross-sectional data set that was collected purposely to examine juvenile delinquency among middle and high school students. All the subjects from the U.S. sample were recruited from one public middle and one public high school in Largo, Florida. New data for this study were collected from students in Taiwan who were enrolled in a junior and a senior high school in one school district of Taiwan's second largest city (Kaohsiung).

U.S. sample

    The U.S. data were collected in Largo, Florida, in 1998. Largo is a metropolitan area comprising 17.9 square miles and located about 23 miles west of Tampa. Its population during the 1990s was around 69,000 people: 47% male, 92% white, and 16% younger than 18 years (U.S. Census Bureau, 1990, 2000). About 6% of Largo's families had incomes below the poverty level, and the city's 1998 median adjusted household income was $42,000 (Largo Chamber of Commerce, 1998; U.S. Census Bureau, 1990,

2000). In 1998, the city's official crime rate (per 100,000) was 5,019 (Florida Department of Law Enforcement, 1999).

The Largo middle school, one of the two area middle schools (grades 6-8), enrolled 1,294 students during the 1998-1999 school year; the average class size was 25 students. Students from all Social Studies classes were invited to participate. Before the actual survey, a passive parental consent form was distributed to students (see Verrill, 2008 for details). On the day of the survey, a researcher explained the purpose of the study to all participants, reminded students that participation was voluntary, and reassured them of the confidentiality of all the information they gave. The researcher then remained on site to answer questions related to the survey. The final response rate was 81% (N = 1,049).

The Largo public high school, one of several high schools (grades 9-12) in this area, enrolled about 1,848 students during the 1998-1999 school year; the average class size was 33 students. As in the Largo middle school survey, a passive parental consent procedure was used. Students from a random sample of 30 third-period school classes were asked to participate. On the day of administration, a researcher described the purpose of the study, explained that participation was voluntary and that the provided information was confidential, and remained available to answer questions (Wareham, Cochran, Sellers, & Dembo, 2005). The final response rate was 79% (n = 625).

Taiwanese sample

The additional data for this study were collected from a sample of junior and senior high school students in Kaohsiung, which comprises about 59.3 square miles and has a population of about 1.5 million: 49.4% male, 21% 18 or younger, and with a marriage rate of about 4.78 per 1, 000 (Department of Budget, Accounting and Statistics, Kaohsiung City Government, 2009). The city's average family income was $38,832[19] in 2009, and about 1.5% of Kaohsiung's families were considered low income by the city government (Department of Budget, Accounting and Statistics, Kaohsiung City Government, 2009). The overall 2009 official crime rate (per 100,000) of Kaohsiung was 1,317 and the juvenile crime rate was 967[20] (Department of Budget, Accounting and Statistic, Kaohsiung City Government, 2009). The city has neither a remarkable concentration of particular demographic groups nor a high crime area in any of its 11 districts.

The Zuo-Ying district, one of the 11 districts, has a rich historical background and is an important military harbor of Taiwan. With a high speed rail station and rapid transit system that were built in recent years, it has become an important business hub of the northern part of Kaohsiung. The Zuo-Ying district comprises 7.48 square miles and has a population of about 189,944: 49% male and about 25% age 18 or younger (Department of Budget, Accounting and Statistics, Kaohsiung City Government, 2009).

---

[19] This number is based on 1 (U.S. Dollar): 29 (NT Dollar) exchange rate.

[20] The number here represents number of offenders per 100, 000 in Kaohsiung City.

The selection of Taiwanese junior and senior high school students comparable to those in the U.S. survey was not easy, because of educational and political system differences. For example, Taiwan has 23 prefectures and two municipal cities with populations over 1 million (Taipei and Kaohsiung city), and all of these prefectures and municipal cities are under the central government's control. In contrast, the U.S. has 50 states, each of which has its own laws and independent political systems. In Taiwan, a junior high school education is compulsory, but a senior high school education is not; also, education systems offer three years of education. In the U.S., education in middle (junior) school lasts for three years, but senior high school offers 4 years of education. However, despite these differences, both Largo and the Zuo-Ying district are similar in many ways. For example, both selected areas are near a coast and a metropolitan area (Largo to Tampa; Zuo-Ying to Kaohsiung city), and the selected schools are similar in size and geographic location (i.e., all in the same school district). Hence, the study attempted in various ways to make the two samples comparable.

The junior high school selected for the present study from the Zuo-Ying district was Zuo-Ying junior high school. There are five public junior high schools in the Zuo-Ying district, and these junior high schools vary in size compared to the average number of students in Kaohsiung City (Education Bureau, Kaohsiung City, 2010). Specifically, three schools are relatively large with over 2,200 students each, one is in the middle range with over 1,000 students and one is small, with only about 400 students. The Zuo-Ying junior high school is one of the three large schools in this district, similar in size to the Largo public middle school. The age range of junior high school students in Taiwan as a whole is 12-15. The total number of students in the Zuo-Ying junior high school was 2,265 in 2010: male students constituted about 51% (n = 1,153), and the average class size was 37 students (Education Bureau, Kaohsiung City, 2010).

In order to collect all subjects (junior and senior high school students) from the same district, as the Largo study did, the senior high school sample was also selected from the Zuo-Ying district. Of the approximately 27[21] senior high schools in Kaohsiung City, 4 are in the Zuo-Ying district; of these four, two are public high schools and two are affiliated private senior high schools. Each of the two public senior high school has over 1,700 students, which is slightly more than the average for public senior high schools (n = 1,546) (Education Bureau, Kaohsiung City, 2010). The Zuo-Ying senior high school that was selected for the present study enrolled 1,789 students in 2010, with 48% male students (n = 867) and an average class size of 35 (Education Bureau, Kaohsiung City, 2010). Compared to the Largo public high school, the Zuo-Ying senior high school has slightly fewer students.

In Taiwan, a junior and senior high school student usually goes to his or her homeroom every day where he or she will be with all those who will be classmates for three school years. Almost all the major school subjects are taught by different teachers in the homeroom, except some special subjects, such as music or physical education. In addition students will need to decide their future track[22] before starting their first year of

---

[21] Among these 27 senior high schools, 5 are private senior high schools, and 5 of all public and 2 of all private senior high schools are affiliated senior high schools.

[22] The first track is geared toward language (e.g., Chinese, English), law, or business schools in universities. The second track is geared toward medical school, social science (e.g., sociology, psychology), engineering

senior high school. The subjects taught will be the same for all students in a given track. Hence, unlike the situation in the Largo high school, in which random samples of students had been selected from 30 third-period high school classes, classes from each track and grade were selected in order to have enough students[23]. Although the principals of the selected schools provided support letters to the research team, they still showed concern about letting "outsiders" into school during regular school hours. A compromise was reached whereby the principals agreed to supply teachers to help in administering the survey by distributing the survey and then remaining on site to help answer questions[24]. All students present on the day of the survey were given opportunity to participate, but because of the voluntary nature of this survey, not all students present on the day participated[25]. Before the day of survey administration, students received two letters from the teacher: one letter explained the purpose of the study, indicated that participation was voluntary, and the researchers would assure that no student names would be placed on survey forms; the second letter, a passive parental consent letter, described the research

---

school (e.g., electronic engineering, mechanic engineering), and other schools in universities (e.g., biology, veterinary medicine). The curricula are, therefore, different except for some fundamental courses (e.g., math, Chinese).

[23] Enough students means that the study planned to collect a similar number of students as the Largo study had. The Largo study had 625 high school students and 1,049 middle school students, thus, this study decided to recruit about this same number.

[24] Students might have been unwilling to respond to sensitive questions (e.g., delinquency) because teachers were on site. Compared to other self-report studies in Taiwan where teachers were not on scene, the proportion of students who reported delinquency in this study was not particularly low. For example, about 12% and 27% of students had purposely damaged property and used alcohol in the present study. The number was 17% and 20% respectively in Tung's research project in 2000. Similarly, the number was 9.5% and 10.2% respectively in a government research report, which was based on a representative sample of Taiwanese youths in 2003.

[25] The participating rate is 91% (860 students out of 945 students) for the Zuo-Ying senior high school, and the rate is 96% (960 students out of 999 students) for the Zuo-Ying junior high school.

and stated the exact day and time of the survey. In addition to these letters, the first page of the survey again assured all students that the survey information would be kept anonymous and that the information would be available only to the researchers.

The survey questionnaire was mainly developed in English and for research in the U.S. Hence, some procedural problems must be addressed before further discussion of the survey. Van de Vijver and Leung (1997, pp. 31-35) pointed out some pitfalls in the cross-cultural research procedure. Briefly, these can be summarized as follows: the researcher is unfamiliar with the target culture, the subjects in the target culture are unfamiliar with the response procedures, and there are differences in the sample. The fact that the present researcher is from the target culture reduces the first problem. The second problem can be dealt with through a pretest (van de Vijver & Leung, 1997). The pretest with a small sample of Taiwanese 7th graders indicated no problem with reading and understanding. The response categories are familiar to Taiwanese adolescents, because many research projects conducted in Taiwan have employed similar response choices (e.g., Taiwan Youth Project) and because public polls also use these response options. In addition, the present researcher and other Ph.D. students from Taiwan reviewed the entire survey instrument. This procedure helped to identify items that did not make sense or seemed awkward to Taiwanese readers, which could cause problems related to stimulus characteristics. For example, although marijuana may be a common substance used by students in America, Ketamine or MDMA are the substances that Taiwanese students most often use.

105

Besides the above mentioned pitfalls that might plague research procedures in cross-cultural research, method bias can also occur. Some common method biases are: response familiarity, differences in physical conditions during administration, and communication bias (van de Vijver & Leung, 1997). The first and last biases were reduced as discussed in the previous paragraph. Physical conditions were made as similar as possible across the two cultural samples by having surveys administered during regular class hours in the regular classroom and by using a paper-pencil format for both samples.

Survey preparation

The instrument used in the Taiwan survey is an adaptation of that used in the Largo schools. "Adaptation" refers to the literal translation of the original instrument with some wording and content changes, in order to enhance the appropriateness of such an instrument in a different culture (van de Vijver & Leung, 1997). One important issue that most cross-cultural studies face is the equivalence of the instrument. The most common remedy is back-translation (Brislin, 1986; Hofstede, 2001), which although reducing errors of translation, does not guarantee a perfect or error-free translation (Hofstede, 2001; Sanchez, Spector, & Cooper, 2005). Other steps can be employed to reduce the "variance" left unsolved by back-translation, including the use of translators who not only understand both languages, but also have considerable deep experience with both cultures (Hofstede, 2001; Sanchez et al., 2005). This can provide a more accurate translation that carries the same meanings of the items into different cultures.

The official language in Taiwan is Mandarin; hence, all the survey items adapted from the U.S. study were translated into that language. Five steps were employed to ensure the accuracy of the translation. First, all survey items in the English version were translated into Mandarin by the author. Second, the same version was translated into Mandarin by two doctoral students from Taiwan, who were studying at U.S. universities. Third, the resolution of any differences between the two translated Mandarin versions occurred through discussion between all these doctoral students and the author. Fourth, the consensus Mandarin version was back-translated by a professional bilingual translator. Finally, the differences between the original English version and the back-translated English version were resolved through an in-depth discussion between the author and the translator. The final version of the survey instrument resulted from this discussion.

After the language issue of the survey had been resolved, the final version of the survey was converted to a scantron format, to reduce as much as possible errors that occur while inputting raw data into a computer. Two incidents occurred during the time period of collecting all the scantron sheets and performing final data inputs. First, a flood during that time damaged about fifty of the answered scantron sheets; fortunately, the flood damage was minor enough that all answer sheets were recovered. Second, many students changed their answers, which caused a problem of data reading by the scanner. With regard to the second problem, the researcher and the research assistants were able to go through all the answer sheets to correct these errors, thus reducing to a minimum the possible errors in the final data set.

<u>Measurement of variables</u>

The present study intends not only to apply GST to the study of juvenile delinquency in Taiwan, but also to compare and contrast the GST model between the U.S. and Taiwan. Consequently, the instruments used to measure all variables were identical across the two samples, except for some slight changes made to fit Taiwan's social conditions (e.g., marijuana is substituted by Ketamine or MDMA).

Both of the central components of GST are included: strain and negative emotions. To capture each concept of strain and negative emotion, the survey items were subjected to exploratory factor analysis (EFA) and, based on the results, a composite score was created for each individual strain variable. Two sets of variables, delinquency (which includes three different kinds of delinquent acts[26]) and physical aggression against siblings, were used as the main endogenous variables. Finally, the present study also incorporated two demographic variables (age and gender) as covariates. All these variables were included in the final path analysis.

Delinquency[27]

Juvenile delinquency is defined broadly in the present study. It includes behavior that is prohibited by law as well as acts carried out by youths who are within certain age

---

[26] Three delinquent acts were chosen mainly because these three delinquent acts have enough variation and are theoretically relevant. Detail is given in the delinquency section.

[27] All but two items used in both the U.S. and Taiwanese surveys were worded identically. The two items with different wording are about using marijuana and stealing a car or motorcycle. Marijuana is not common for use by juveniles in Taiwan; the more "popular" substances used are Ketamine and MDMA. In Taiwan, the most common private means of transportation for juveniles are motorcycles and bicycles. Consequently, the item "stealing a car or motorcycle" was changed to "stealing a motorcycle or a bicycle."

limits (e.g., 12-18) (Short & Hughes, 2008; Trojanowicz, Morash, & Schram, 2001). In other words, delinquency refers to behavior that violates the law but is carried out by minors (e.g., damaging property), and also to behavior that is prohibited to youth but not to adults (e.g., alcohol use) (Stafford, 2004).

Self-reported delinquent behaviors included in the present study are fairly commonly reported in the criminological literature (Elliott, Huizinga, & Ageton, 1985; Piquero, Macintosh, & Hickman, 2002). The questionnaire asked students to report whether they have done each of several delinquent acts. However, close examination of these items revealed that for many items, less than 1% of subjects endorsed the acts in both countries; this was especially true in Taiwan. Hence, these items were discarded because of lack of variance to be explained. We finally chose 3 delinquent acts as our outcome variables. These variables not only have relatively high percentages of students reporting that they had done the acts in the past 12 months, but also were theoretically relevant and representative of the general delinquency categories (e.g., property crime, violent crime). For example, we included alcohol use, which is a substance offense and which has been found to be related to strain (Aseltine & Gore, 2000).

The 3 selected delinquent acts are "purposely damage property" (property delinquent act), "hit someone with intention to hurt them" (violent offense), and "alcohol use" (substance use). Individuals who report they have not committed a particular act receive a score of 0, and students who report that they have received a score of 1 (See Appendix A for detailed wording). Each of these three delinquent acts is examined separately because they represent different domains of acts, and Agnew (2006a, 2006b)

109

has advocated separating various coping behaviors by type of act. This analysis helps to identify strain-delinquent specific relationships.

Physical aggression

Card and colleagues (2008) refer to physical aggression as direct aggression (Xie, Farmer, & Cairns, 2003), although direct aggression includes physical and verbal aggression. The present study defines physical aggression as direct confrontation between perpetrator and victims by any physical means (e.g., hitting or kicking) (Xie et al., 2003). Students were asked to report how many times they had engaged in physically aggressive behavior against a sibling in the past 12 months. Notice that one of the response categories is "no siblings." Students who indicated that they had no siblings were dropped. Although this might reduce sample size, the reduction was relatively small for both countries (7.8%, or 117 subjects, for the U.S.; 6.1%, or 106 subjects, for Taiwan). In addition, the analysis for physical aggression was done separately from that for delinquency; hence, the reduction of sample size did not affect other analyses (see Table 2 for the frequency distribution for delinquency and aggression).

Strain

General strain theory (GST) identified strain as relationships in which the "individual is not treated as he or she wants to be" (Agnew, 1992, p. 48). Later, Agnew (2006a) defined strain as "events or conditions that are disliked by individuals" (p.4). The present study adopts the latter definition because it is broader and more inclusive.

Agnew (1992) outlined three major types of strain: failure to achieve positively valued goals, removal of positively valued stimuli, and presentation of noxious stimuli. For the first kind of strain, the present study includes measures of (1) the discrepancy between desired goals and actual outcomes and. Stressful life-events involving loss (3) were used as a measure of the second type of strain. Finally, (4) victimization was used as a measure of the presentation of negative stimuli (see Appendix A for detailed wording).

The purpose of the study was to investigate the effects of these four different strains on subsequent delinquency. Consequently, a composite score was created for each of the strain variables. To ensure that all items being used are reasonably able to "hang together" for both countries, we conducted exploratory factor analysis (EFA) for each strain variable. The present study used principal axis factoring (PAF), which is the mostly widely used method, instead of principal components analysis (PCA) to conduct EFA for two reasons[28].

First, EFA is aimed at explaining community (i.e., variance shared by items or indicators) of the correlations among all items used to measure latent concepts, and thus is highly consistent with the goal of determining whether the items used in the present study could be accounted for by the underlying latent concept (e.g., anger). Many scholars have suggested that when the goal of analysis is to identify a latent construct, one should use EFA rather than PCA (Fabriga, Wegener, MacCallum, & Strahan, 1999; Gorsuch, 1983). In addition, it is necessary, though not sufficient, to demonstrate that the

---

[28] The discussion that is followed focuses on the difference between EFA in general and PCA. The intention is to clarify the confusions between EFA and PCA and the justification of using EFA. PAF is one of many EFA methods, and the discussion can apply to PAF.

latent concept (factor) accounts for the common relationship among a set of indicators, before the validity of the construct, the model, and the indicator can be accepted (Pedhazur & Schmelkin, 1991). In contrast, PCA extracts components that account for as much variance as possible, and it does not differentiate between common variance and unique variance. Moreover, the extracted components are not latent concepts. For these reasons, Fabriga et al. (1999, p.275) stated that PCA "is not a factor analysis at all."

Second, and related, the main diagonal of the matrix analyzed in EFA consists of commonality, which usually is not equal to one. This is important because this does not assume error-free measurement. Unlike EFA, PCA treats the main diagonal of the matrix as error-free; that is, it puts unity at the main diagonal. This is counterintuitive, because most social science research contains random error. Consequently, the present study uses the principal axis factoring approach to EFA as a guide to create the conceptual variables.

One of the controversies surrounding EFA is with the regard to how many factors should be retained. Although some statistical guidelines exist for this matter (e.g., Kaiser-criterion), criticism of these rules persist. Pedhazur and Schmelkin (1991) argued that decisions on EFA (e.g., number of factors to retain) should be "made within a theoretical context" (p.622). Following their admonition, this study used theory as the guideline to decide on the number of factors to retain. In each EFA, we retained only one factor, because the GST would predict that the items should reasonably represent a single underlying theoretical construct. This decision later was supported by the statistical rules;

that is, the scree plot combined with the Kaiser-criterion agreed with the 1 factor solution for each of the EFAs[29] (the factor loadings in Appendix B).

After conducting EFA, the study created the composite score for each strain variable. Two different scoring procedures were used. For goal strain and unjust strain, all the items are on the ordinal level; hence, we divided each item by its own standard deviation (SD) before summing all items together, rather than summing z-scores for each item. By doing this, we avoided two problems. First, as when using z-scores, dividing the raw score by its SD prevents assigning too much weight to items that have great variance; there is no theoretical reason to believe that some items should have greater weight than others. Second, dividing a raw score by its SD, rather than using a z-score which subtracts the mean from the raw score before dividing by its SD, preserves the mean differences across countries; this is important because one purpose of this study was to discover whether there is a difference between the two countries. For the negative life-event (10 items) and victimization scale (6 items), each item has only 2 categories; hence, a z-score was created for each individual item and then the z-scores were summed to create a composite score for each of these two strain variables.

---

[29] The present study conducted six EFAs, four for strain variables and 2 for negative emotions. In each of these analyses, each item loaded over .4 (Pedhazur & Schmelkin, 1991) on its respective factors. In some cases the loadings were not over .4 but greater than .3; these items were still included because of theoretical expectations. Moreover, the cut-off on loading is still much debated and subjective; some researchers would accept .3 as a reasonable cut-off point (Child, 2006).

Failure to achieve positively valued goals—disjunction between desired and actual outcome. Agnew (1992) criticized classic strain theories (Merton, 1938; Cohen, 1955; Cloward & Ohlin, 1960) because they focus only on blockage of long-term monetary goals. Later researchers argued that, although monetary goals are important, a juvenile may have goals other than money, such as popularity and autonomy (Agnew, 1985; Agnew, 2006a). The present study covers various goals that a youth might find important in his or her current life (e.g., relationships, autonomy). Specifically, students were asked to evaluate whether they strongly agree, agree, disagree, or strongly disagree with several statements regarding receiving respect from parents and teachers (3 items), relationships with others (2 items), and autonomy (2 items). Higher scores indicate that students did not achieve or were unsatisfied with their situation regarding these goals and hence experienced greater strain.

Failure to achieve positively valued goals—unjust outcomes. According to GST, strain may be the result of a disjunction between a desired goal and an actual achievement, as when an individual focuses on achieving but fails to attain a specific outcome (e.g., popularity). Another possible and related source of a strain is when an individual enters into a relationship with the expectation that a certain rule of justice will be followed. Agnew (1992) argued that a relationship is most stressful if the outcome/input ratio is not equal, when individuals feel they have been under-rewarded (Hegtvedt, 1990). To capture these feelings of unjust strain, seven items asked students whether they agree or disagree with statements about unequal relationships in which they are involved. For example, students can choose from strongly agree to strongly disagree in response to the statement,

114

"Many students don't study as hard as I do, but they still make better grades." Although these items do not specify the exact input/output ratio of all involved parties, all the statements delineate clearly a situation in which the respondent does not "get the best deal" (Agnew, 1992). Higher scores indicated greater unjust strain (see Table B1 in Appendix B for factor loadings for both variables).

Loss of positive stimuli–negative life-events. Strain can be a result of losing a positively valued goal (Agnew, 1992). The most widely used instrument that captures this type of strain and the presentation of negative stimuli, whether in the stress literature (Kaplan, 1983; Thoits, 1983) or in studies that examine GST (Eitle & Turner, 2003; Hoffmann & Miller, 1997; Mazerolle & Piquero, 1997) is the negative life-event scale. Although many different negative life-event scales exist, Turner and Wheaton (1995) argue that there is no advantage in using one particular scale rather than another and that scales should be tailored to fit the studied population (Herbert & Cohen, 1996). In addition, these authors also suggest that a 1-year time frame should be used and unweighted indices are as useful as any (Herbert & Cohen, 1996). The negative life-event scale (10 items) used in the present study has all of the four recommended features, and all events are related to loss of positive stimuli (e.g., death of a relative, loss of a friendship). Students reported whether the event had happened to them (yes = 1) in the past 12 months or not (no = 0). Higher scores indicate that a student experienced many stressful life-events and consequently had a higher level of strain.

Presentation of noxious stimuli–victimization. Noxious stimuli by definition are those events or incidents that are disliked by individuals. Criminal victimization is one of the

115

most severe noxious stimuli and types of strain. Here, victimization refers to any physical, mental (emotional), and financial harm people suffer because of the criminal activities of others (Karmen, 2001). Six different victimizations were used to tap into this strain, such as being forced to give up money or possessions or being physically attacked by others. Students were asked to indicate whether they have experienced an incident in the past 12 months (yes = 1) or have not (no = 0). Higher scores indicate a higher level of strain.

Negative emotion

Emotion refers to a person's response, after cognitive evaluation, to a stimulus (e.g., an event, an object, or a person) related to his or her concerns or goals (Lazarus, 1991). Negative emotions, then, are present or felt when advancement of goals or concerns is impeded. Simply put, a negative emotion reflects a gap between an ideal goal and an actual goal (Larson & Asmussen, 1991; Lazarus, 1999; Solomon, 1976), and matches well with GST.

The present study measures two important negative emotions: anger and depression. The former, a central negative emotion in GST, is regarded as an outer-directed emotion (Agnew, 1992; Jang & Johnson, 2003). The latter has gained increased interest in research on GST because Agnew (2006a, 2006b) suggested that researchers should pay more attention to other negative emotions, such as depression, an inner-directed emotion (Ganem, 2008; Jang & Johnson, 2003).

Anger. Eight items were used to measure anger, five of which are adopted from Spielberger's (1988) State-Trait Anger Expression Inventory (STAXI), which examines

116

anger as a personality trait that is situational (Wareham et al., 2005). One example of these five items is "When I get frustrated, I feel like hitting others." The other three items capture angry feelings or reactions that are also more situational. One example is "It makes me mad when I don't get the respect from others that I deserve." These eight items appear to be primarily situational, which is in tandem with the suggestions of Agnew and others (2006a; Baron, 2004; Mazerolle et al., 2003). Response categories were coded so that a higher score indicates a higher level of anger (see Table B2 in Appendix B for factor loadings for both anger and depression).

Depression. Four items are used to measure depression. In contrast to the anger measures, which are more situational, these four items appear to be trait-like or symptoms of depression. This may incur criticism because currently GST advocates use of measures that tap into situational emotions. Three reasons may justify such use. First, most measures of depression in psychology are similar to the present items, which capture symptoms of depression, whether physical or behavioral (e.g., CES-D scale, Radloff, 1977). Second, studies that claim to measure situational distress/depression use similar items/symptoms. The difference is that they ask respondents to answer questions based on when they were experiencing strain. Third, in an even more direct measure of situational depression by using vignettes, Ganem (2008) failed to capture pure situational depression, in that respondents reported other emotions along with depression. Hence, capturing situational depression may not be as easy as one would think, and without more sophisticated strategies, one may measure negative emotions other than depression.

117

The four depression items to be used in the present study are adopted from the Beck Depression Inventory, second edition (BDI-II) (Beck, Steer, & Brown, 1996). These items ask students to indicate how often the following statements describe them. (1) I don't look forward to things as much as I used to, (2) I find it hard to keep my mind on school work, (3) I sleep very well (reverse coded), and (4) I have lots of energy (reverse coded). These four items include both a somatic component of depression (the last two items) and an affective component of depression (the first two items) (Storch, Roberti, & Roth, 2004). The response categories are identical to that of the anger measure (see Appendix A for detailed wording). A higher score indicates a greater level of depression.

One caution must be presented here. The EFA results indicated that a 1 factor solution is acceptable in the U.S. sample because the loading of these four items were all over .4 except the first item, which had loading at .349. In contrast, these four items did not load evenly in the Taiwanese sample, with the first two items having very low loadings (see Table B2 in Appendix B for detail). However, the eigen value (sum of squared loadings) was over 1 for the Taiwanese sample. Thus, this study still treated depression as one factor in Taiwan so that the model construct was similar across the two countries. The difference is due to the high correlation between the two somatic items in the Taiwanese sample, but not in the U.S. sample. One possible explanation is that Chinese people have the tendency to identify physical illness but report psychological discomfort relatively seldom. This phenomenon, called somatization, refers to people who emphasize physical symptoms of depression more than psychological ones (Heine, 2010). Moreover, in Chinese society, psychological illness incurs a great deal of stigma;

hence, the results obtained here would be expected in the Taiwan sample. However, to make the model construct similar across the two countries, the present study still treated depression as one factor for both samples (see Table 2 for the descriptive statistics for strain, anger, and depression).

Demographic variables

The present study includes two important demographic variables, gender and age, that have been shown to influence the strain-delinquency relationship. Studies have shown that males and females may have different reactions and coping strategies under strain/stress (Hoffmann & Su, 1997; Mirowsky & Ross, 1995; Perlin, 1989; Piquero & Sealock, 2000; Sharp et al., 2005; Thoits, 1995; Van Gundy, 2002). *Gender* is therefore included in the survey, with male coded 1 and female is coded 0. *Age* is also included (students' age on the date of the survey), because as individuals grow older, they may accumulate different experiences, and develop different responses to strain and different coping skills (Hauser & Bowlds, 1990; Petersen, Kennedy, & Sullivan, 1991; Thoits, 1995; Turner, Wheaton, & Donald, 1995).

Race is not considered as a control variable because in Taiwan, there is essentially no "minority group," except for some aboriginal individuals who constitute only 2% of the total population (Directorate-General of Budget, Accounting, and Statistics, Executive Yuan, Taiwan, 2010). One recent trend is an increase in numbers of so-called "New Taiwanese Children," children whose parents are not both Taiwanese. Usually the mother is from another country (e.g., China, Vietnam), because the father is of relatively

119

low SES and thus has difficulty finding a mate in Taiwan. However, according to the Ministry of Education (2009), in 2008, junior high school students from such families comprised only 1% of the total junior high student population. Consequently, race is not included as a covariate in the subsequent analysis for either sample (see Table 3 for the frequency distribution for the two demographic variables).

Table 2 Descriptive Statistics of Strain and Negative Emotion Variables

	U.S.(N = 1,516)		Taiwan (N = 1,717)	
Variable	Mean[1]	SD[2]	Mean	SD
Goal strain	15.03	3.70	14.57	4.13
Unjust strain	16.84	3.96	19.10	4.10
Life-event[3]	0	4.97	0	5.25
Victimization	0	3.21	0	3.20
Anger	19.37	4.92	17.58	5.14
Depression	8.7	2.60	9.34	2.54

[1]The reported mean is the average mean across the 5 datasets.

[2] The reported SD is the average SD across the 5 datasets.

[3]The means of Life-event and victimization scale are 0 because of standardization.

Table 3 Frequency Distribution of Demographic Variables, Aggression, and Delinquency

		U.S.			Taiwan	
Gender	n	%	Mean (SD)	n	%	Mean (SD)
Male	730	48.2%	.480	844	49.2%	.490
Female	786	51.8%	(.500)	873	50.8%	(.500)
Total	1,516	100%		1,717	100%	
Age						
11	185	12.2%				
12	288	19%		93	5.4%	
13	317	20.9%		452	26.3%	
14	209	13.8%		306	17.8%	
15	155	10.2%	13.780	383	22.3%	14.630
16	185	12.2%	(1.984)	150	8.7%	(1.604)
17	125	8.2%		297	17.3%	
18	46	3%		31	1.8%	
19	6	.4%		5	.3%	
Total	1,516	100%		1,717	100%	
Damage property						
Yes	206	13.6%	.140	203	11.8%	.120
No	1,310	86.4%	(.343)	1,514	88.2%	(.323)
Total	1,516	100%		1,717	100%	
Hit someone						
Yes	357	24.5%	.230	122	7.1%	.070
No	1,159	75.5%	(.424)	1,595	92.9%	(.257)
Total	1,516	100%		1,717	100%	
Alcohol use						
Yes	575	37.9%	.380	474	27.6%	.280
No	941	62.1%	(.485)	1,243	72.4%	(.447)
Total	1,516	100%		1,717	100%	
Aggression[12]						
Never	524	37.6%		1,104	68.6%	
1	205	14.7%		159	9.9%	
2	140	10.1%	2.000	107	6.6%	2.030
3-5times	156	11.2%	(1.819)	96	6%	(1.635)
6 or more times	367	26.4%		144	8.9%	
Total	1,392	100%		1,610	100%	

[1]The total number of aggression is not the same because of deleting those who have no siblings.

[2]There is 5 missing cases in the U.S. sample and 1 in the Taiwan sample. These missing cases were deleted.

Analytic strategy

Statistical method

The first purpose of the present study was to evaluate the GST model in the U.S. and Taiwan. To achieve this, the study uses path analysis to test the basic GST model in the U.S. and Taiwanese samples (see Figure 1)[30]. Using path analysis as a vehicle to examine the research questions presented in Chapter IV has three advantages. First, path analysis is commonly used to identify causal relationships and to test theoretical models among manifest (observed) variables (Hatcher, 1994; Kline, 2005; Raykov & Marcoulides, 2000).

Second, this statistical technique belongs to the family of structural equation modeling (SEM)[31]; hence, many statistical estimations (e.g., ML, WLS) and methods (e.g., multiple group comparison) may be applied to path analysis. Third, the GST model also specifies mediating effects among theoretical variables, and James and Brett (1984) suggest that researchers must use path analytic techniques to assess mediation. Baron and Kenny (1986) likewise recommend path modeling to test mediation, noting that the method allows simultaneous testing of all relevant paths.

---

[30] The correlation between anger and depression was added because previous studies had found that negative emotions were likely to co-occurred (Ganem, 2008; Sharp et al., 2001).

[31] The SEM family includes several statistical models: path analysis models of observed variables, confirmatory factor analysis models that examine the non-causal pattern of relationships among latent constructs, structural regression models that specify causal relationships among latent constructs, and latent growth models that examine effects over time (Kline, 2005; Raykov & Marcoulides, 2000).

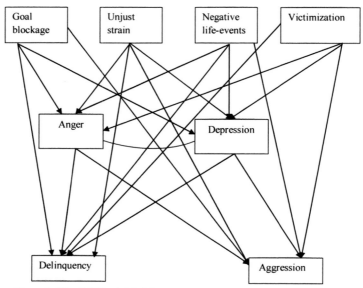

Figure 1. The GST Path Model

To achieve the second purpose of the present study, that of comparing and contrasting the GST model across countries, a SEM multiple-groups approach was used. In conventional statistics, such as ANOVA, the group difference is estimated by a categorical variable, which represents group membership (e.g., a dummy gender variable). However, such a comparison is limited to mean difference; that is, delinquent boys, for instance, have more delinquent friends than non-delinquent boys have. Other possible differences, such as different processes, are ignored. Another conventional approach is to fit the same model across different groups. That is, the same model was tested separately in each group. Although this method provides a flexible approach to comparing groups, it is also limited. For example, when a particular path is compared across groups, a

123

statistically significant result can indicate that a difference is present. However, this test provides information on a difference rather than on a similarity. Hence, finding that estimates are not significantly different, does not mean these parameters are the same (Maruyama, 1997). For example, one might use Paternoster and colleagues' (1998) equation to compare the path coefficients across male (b1) and female (b2) samples. The z-score from this equation can provide information regarding whether b1 = b2. However, like other significance tests, rejecting the null hypothesis does not mean one can accept the alternative hypothesis because information is lacking on the type II error or power. Moreover, the separate analyses each have lower statistical power. In contrast to these conventional approaches, multiple-groups analysis in the SEM framework provides great flexibility, offering direct comparisons across different groups on various parameters (e.g., path coefficients, group means), and the comparisons reveal not only differences but also similarities. For example, to test similarities, one can impose equality constraints on paths across samples; if such constraint does not make the fit of the model worse, then similarity is confirmed. In contrast, freeing one path provides the test for differences. In addition, this approach utilizes all the subjects from all groups, which provides greater statistical power. The sample size of both groups in the present study is over 1,500, which is considered large by various statistical standards, and Maruyama (1997, p.259) argued that with sufficiently large samples[32], "modeling groups as multiple populations is a superior alternative to dummy coding."

---

[32] The argument here is to justify the use of multiple-groups analysis, not to devalue the MIMIC (multiple indicators, multiple causes) approach. MIMIC is a valuable alternative to multiple-groups analysis. It has several advantages: it is parsimonious and it requires fewer samples.

Two points must be mentioned here before discussing missing data. First, contrary to the requirements of regular SEM and path analysis models, which employ ML (maximum likelihood estimation) and assume multivariate normality, the delinquent acts in this study are all dichotomized variables, which violate the normality assumption. Hence, regular ML estimation might be problematic. Although research has indicated that ML is robust to minor departures from normality (Chou & Bentler, 1995), Brown (2006) argued that when categorical data are encountered, ML should never be used. One popular alternative estimator is weighted least squares (WLS), which adjusts the weight matrix (W) by taking into account multivariate kurtosis in the variance/covariance matrix. Brown (2006) argued that WLS does not perform well with small samples, and other researchers also report that WLS does not provide proper estimations with the use of categorical outcome variables (Flora & Curran, 2004). One proper alternative estimator is weighted least square mean and variance (WLSMV), which is used to account for non-normality. Flora and Curran (2004) have shown that WLSMV is an accurate estimator when sample sizes vary from 100 to 1,000 with various degrees of non-normality and model complexity. Each sample in the present study has more than 1,500 subjects; hence, employing WLSMV as the estimator seems appropriate.

Second, several indirect effects are examined in the path model. Although the traditional method is to use the Baron and Kenny (1986) approach or the Sobel test (1982), simulation studies reveal that these two procedures perform poorly compared with other modern methods (e.g., bootstrapping) (Fritz & MacKinnon, 2007; MacKinnon, Lockwood, Hoffman, West, & Sheets, 2002). The problem with traditional methods is that the significance of indirect effects is not distributed normally; hence, standard errors and related significance tests are biased. To correct for this bias, bootstrapping can be used. Bootstrapping is a resampling procedure in which the original data are randomly drawn many times with replacement. These resampled samples provide a basis for estimating the parameters of interest. Because of this random drawing with replacement, no distribution assumption is involved. Brown (2006) called the sampling distribution from bootstrapping "concrete." Hence, researchers often suggest that when the assumption of normal-theory statistics is violated, bootstrapping is an attractive alternative (Adèr, Mellenbergh, & Hand, 2008; Brown, 2006). Similarly, a growing literature has advocated using bootstrapping when assessing indirect effects (Bollen & Stine, 1990; Hayes, 2009; MacKinnon, Lockwood, & Williams, 2004).

Missing data

The present study employed two steps to handle missing data. First, students who did not report either their gender or age were excluded from the analysis. For the U.S. sample, about 27 students (1%) failed to report either gender or age, and for the Taiwan sample, about 41 students (2%) did not report either gender or age. After these cases were deleted, the U.S. sample had 1,647 subjects and the Taiwanese sample had 1,779 students. However, further case deletion was done for ease of data imputation. Although multiple imputation (MI) with the Markov Chain Monte Carlo (MCMC) approach can effectively handle data with a high proportion of missing cases, it requires more iterations and generates more complete sets of data, which is computationally intensive. To avoid this problem, this study decided *a priori* that students who failed to report more than 2 items

126

on a scale were excluded from MI. For example, on the victimization scale (7 items), three types of students were excluded from MI: the first type of students omitted all 7 items, the second type of students omitted 6 items, and the last type of students omitted 5 items. This criterion further reduced the U.S. sample to 1,516 and the Taiwanese sample to 1,717[33].

Second, after these cases were deleted, MI (Rubin, 1987) was used to replace the missing values for all items. Although single imputation (e.g., mean replacement), in which only a single value is used to replace the missing value, is easy to implement, two serious disadvantages prevented the present study from employing this method. First, single imputation tends to underestimate standard errors, resulting in greater likelihood of rejecting the null hypothesis. Second, it does not perform well even if the missing data pattern is ignorable (MCAR or MAR). In contrast, MI uses several values to impute the missing value, which results in multiple complete data sets. By using multiple sets of data to estimate parameters of interest, a researcher adds variability into the estimation, which can be used to adjust the standard error upward; that is, in turn it reduces Type I error (McKnight, Mcknight, Sidani, & Figueredo, 2007). It has been shown that MI can be successfully implemented on data missing not at random (MNAR) (Verbeke & Molenberghs, 2000) and provide satisfactory results with minor departures from MAR

---

[33] For the U.S. sample, the negative life-event scale had most missing subjects (n = 73) who did not report more than 2 items on the scale. On the other hand, for the Taiwan sample, the goal strain scale had the most missing cases (n = 31). Other scales (e.g., anger, goal strain) together had 58 missing cases in the U.S. and 31 missing cases in Taiwan.

(Collins, Schafer, & Kam, 2001; Rubin, 1996)[34]. Moreover, this method has become the most highly praised method for statistically dealing with missing cases (Allison, 2002; Rubin, 1996; Shafer & Graham, 2002; McKnight et al., 2007), and is the dominant model of handling missing data (Abraham & Russell, 2004). In addition, Rubin (1996) indicated that MI not only provides generalizable estimates but also recovers variance for statistical inference. On the basis of such literature support, using MI seemed to be justifiable and appropriate.

MI with the MCMC approach is used in the present study. The advantage of using the MCMC approach is that it can easily handle almost every kind of underlying distribution; McKnight et al. (2007) have suggested MCMC as one approach to be used when using MI with non-normal data, as in the present study, which has dichotomized variables. Generally, the procedure involves two steps: the imputing (I-step) and the posterior (P-step). The I-step starts with an estimated mean and covariance matrix and simulates a missing value for each observable data point. The P-step begins with the complete data from the I-step and then generates a mean and covariance matrix based on the posterior distribution[35]. The generated mean and covariance matrix from the P-step is, then, used for the next I-step. The iteration between the I-step and P-step creates a Markov chain with the goal of creating a distribution of missing data, from which missing values are randomly drawn.

---

[34] In contrast this positive reference, Sinharay, Stern, and Russell (2001) indicated MI provided improved estimation but it is still biased.
[35] A posterior distribution is a distribution that is adjusted and updated based on information gained from observing data.

Before imputing missing values, both datasets were submitted to the Little's (1988) MCAR chi-square test[36], which helped to check whether the missingness of the present data is completely at random (MCAR) or not. For the U.S. sample, the chi-square test result was not significant at the .05 level, χ^2 (2,451, N = 1,516) = 2560, p = .06. This indicated that the missing pattern in the U.S. sample is MCAR and MI is appropriate. In contrast, the chi-square test result for the Taiwanese sample was significant, χ^2 (980, N = 1,717) = 1109, p < .01. A series of comparisons across all the variables between missing and non-missing cases revealed only a few significant differences, which should not be necessarily viewed with caution. First, many comparisons were based on very few missing cases. For example, when considering item4 on the unjust scale and item7 on the anger scale, there are only 8 missing cases. With these few cases, the meaning of any comparison is trivial. Second, the total number of pairs of comparisons is well over 100; after the Bonferroni correction, one would need a p value far below .01 to obtain a significant result. Many of the comparisons are significant at the .05 or .01 level, which may be insignificant when applying the Bonferroni correction. Consequently, the missingness might well be a matter of missing at random (MAR), which is also an acceptable condition for using MI.

Besides the above concerns regarding conducting MI, some other decisions need to be made. First, one must determine the number of iterations needed to achieve two important conditions: (1) the algorithm has converged to the correct distribution and (2)

---

[36] This test compared observed means for each missing pattern with the expected population means, and then, computed an overall weighted squared deviation. The test used the overall weighted squared deviation and tested the null model (e.g., MCAR) by comparing it with the Chi-square distribution.

there is no statistical dependence between the observations in one generated data set and another (Allison, 2003). Allison (2003, p.553) stated that "[U]nfortunately, not much is known about just how many iterations are needed to achieve these aims." Thus, there is no clear rule that can help researchers to make such decisions *a priori*.

For example, Allison (2002) argued that a small portion of missing data may be estimated properly with a small number of iterations, but he did not provide specific numbers. Similarly, Schafer (1997) presented different numbers of iterations, 50 to 1,000, for conducting MI under different situations. Although there is no clear "rule of thumb," Allison (2002) did suggest that the number of iterations should be as large as it would be with use of the EM (expectation maximization) algorithm. He later (Allison, 2003) suggested that the default in the SAS program, 200 burn-in iterations and 100 iterations to generate the first data set, is more than enough for the majority of missing data sets. The present study uses 500 iterations to conduct MI, which is much greater than the number of iterations when EM is used in SPSS[37], and it is also greater than the default mentioned by Allison (2003) in SAS.

The second related issue pertains to the number of complete data sets. The higher the proportion of missing data, the more datasets are required. As mentioned before, the missingness is not greater than 5% in both countries; hence, 2 or more complete datasets should be enough. In fact, Rubin and Schenker (1986) suggested that 2 sets of imputation are enough for missing at 10%. In a later Monte Carlo study, Schafer (1997) reported that

---

[37] The default iteration in SPSS for EM is 25.

even with severe missingness (90% of the data missing), fewer than 20 imputations will be required. The present study used the default, 5 complete data sets, which is usually efficient (Allison, 2003). Schafer and Olsen (1998) have shown that 5 complete data sets produce an efficient estimate even when the proportion of missing information is 50%. In addition, Allison (2003, p.553) stated that 5 imputed data sets is "widely regarded as sufficient[38] for a small to moderate amount of missing data." As mentioned previously, the fraction of missing cases in the present study is less than 5%, which is considered a low amount of missing data. Consequently, 5 data sets are sufficient in the present situation.

Although all these considerations have been taken into account, there is no guarantee that the specified number of iterations would converge, given the large size of the sample of the present study. Fortunately, there are some statistical methods that can be used to determine whether the problem of convergence is present. One simple approach is to plot the parameter values (e.g., mean, SD) against the iteration history (Schafer, 1997). For example, in the present study, the ideal imputation result is that the mean and SD of the items for each scale are not varied across iteration, thus a stable estimation of the mean and SD can be reached. Hence, plotting the mean and SD against iteration history is checked. If there is no clear trend in the plot, then convergence has been achieved. Allison (2002) suggested conducting this inspection on variables that have the most missing values, because these are most likely the variables to be problematic.

---

[38] Efficient is defined "[E]fficiency means that an estimator has a sampling variance that is at least as small as that of any other estimator" (Allison, 2003, p.548, foot note 5).

For the U.S. sample, item 4 of the goal strain scale was selected because it has the largest number of missing cases (n = 37); for the Taiwanese sample, item 7 of the unjust scale was chosen (n = 19). Both plots showed no particular trend; in other words, they appeared to be random (see Figure 2 for the U.S. sample and Figure 3 for the Taiwan sample). This assured that the non-convergence problem was at a minimum.

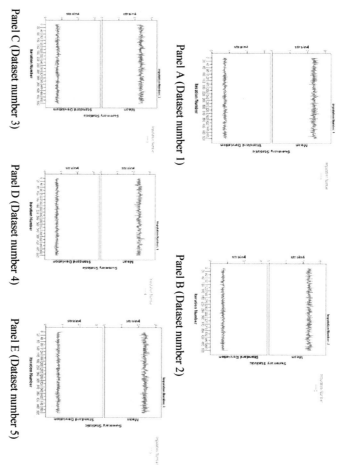

Panel A (Dataset number 1)   Panel B (Dataset number 2)

Panel C (Dataset number 3)   Panel D (Dataset number 4)   Panel E (Dataset number 5)

Figure 2. The Iteration History Plot of Mean and Standard Deviation for the U.S. Sample

133

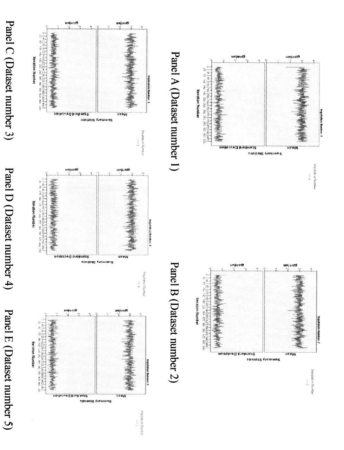

Panel A (Dataset number 1)   Panel B (Dataset number 2)

Panel C (Dataset number 3)   Panel D (Dataset number 4)   Panel E (Dataset number 5)

Figure 3. The Iteration History Plot of Mean and Standard Deviation for the Taiwanese Sample

CHAPTER VI

RESULTS

The analyses that follow use the 5 complete datasets generated by the MI. The first part of this chapter reports the results of applying the GST model in the U.S. sample. The second part of this chapter presents the findings regarding to the Taiwanese sample. The main purpose of these analyses is to examine the GST model, and to answer the research questions of whether strain is related to delinquency and aggression, whether strain is related to anger and depression, and whether strain affects delinquency and aggression through anger and depression. The results also examine whether GST is applicable to Taiwan.

The final part of this chapter provides the results from the multiple group analysis. Although the first two parts examined the GST model, the analyses only focused on whether GST is useful in explaining juvenile delinquency in each country and did not examine the similarities and differences across two countries. With multiple group comparison, the GST model can be further examined to see whether the same relationships found in both countries are truly statistically similar (e.g., imposing constraints). In addition, the multiple group analysis can also provide statistical evaluation of the differences found in the separate analyses (e.g., freeing parameter).

135

One caution must be made here before we turn to reported results. The sample size of each country is well over 1,500, as such, statistically significant path coefficients are likely to be detected. This is because sample size plays a role in null hypothesis significance testing (NHST). The larger the sample size, the greater the ease of rejecting the null hypothesis. As such, many scholars argue that one should not rely on NHST alone but should also focus on substantively significant results[39] (Cohen, 1994; Nakagawa & Cuthill, 2007; Thompson, 1993). In other words, when statistically significant results are almost certain, researchers should turn their attention to practically significant results; that is, the result that has substantive meaning[40]. Applying this thinking to the present case means that the path coefficients that are statistically significant and are relatively large in magnitude are discussed more in the text than path coefficients of relatively small magnitude. This is consistent with Levin (1993) who argued that statistical significance should be built first and then the focus should turn to practical significance.

GST in the U.S.

As previously mentioned, path analysis is adopted to examine the proposed causal relationship among variables. Four outcome variables are incorporated in the analysis: damaging property, hitting someone, alcohol use, and aggression against siblings. GST would predict that students who experience strains should be more likely to commit

---

[39] Substantive results refer to results that have a large effect size. In the present study, the substantive result refers to the relatively large path coefficient, which can be seen as one kind of effect statistic.

[40] The present study proposes the argument here is to justify the reporting practice in this study, but it does not provide all the debates on the issue of effect size and NHST. Interested readers are referred to the whole issue 4 of 1993 *Journal of Experimental Education*.

delinquent acts and aggression and experience negative emotions, such as anger and depression. Table 4 has four models that give the results of the relationship between strain and the four outcome variables. Browsing the results of Table 4, one finds that two types of strain have statistically significant and sizeable effects on the three delinquent acts. Negative life-events is related to damaging property, hitting someone, and alcohol use. This result is consistent with previous reports that negative life-events is related to increased alcohol use and other delinquency among youth (Broidy, 2001; Eitle, 2002; Hoffmann, 2002; Hoffmann & Cerbone, 1999; Hoffmann et al., 2000). The more consistent picture is that victimization has both statistically and substantively significant effects on all four outcome variables. This suggests that victimization, as Agnew (2006a) and previous studies have found (Hay & Evans, 2006; Lin, Cochran, & Mieczkowski, 2011), is a criminogenic strain. Besides these two strains, unjust strain has statistically significant and relatively large effect on hitting someone and aggression against siblings. Goal strain, however, did not have any direct effects on the four outcome variables. Some previous studies have found similar null effects (Broidy, 2001; Moon et al., 2009; Sharp et al., 2005).

Age and gender have different effects on these four outcome variables. For example, older adolescents become involved in alcohol use more often than younger adolescents, which is consistent with previous longitudinal analyses (Aseltine & Gore, 2000). On the other hand, older youth become less involved in aggression against siblings than younger youth. Male students are more likely than female students to hit someone

137

and damage property. Surprisingly, female students report more aggressive behavior and use more alcohol than male students.

Next, we turn to the examination of the relationship between strain and two negative emotions: anger and depression. Figure 4 reveals that all four strain variables have positive and significant effects on anger and depression. Among all the strain variables, goal strain and unjust strain both have the largest statistically significant impact on both anger and depression; that is, students who suffer from goal strain and unjust strain are more likely to experience anger and depressive symptoms than their counterparts who experience less of these two strains. These results provide support for GST. However, Agnew (2006a) encouraged researchers to analyze the specific effect, that is, which particular type of strain is related to which type of negative emotions. For example, he suggested that the "[r]esearcher should also examine whether particular types of strains foster particular negative emotions…" (p.36). The present study, however, did not find support for this statement in that all types of strains were related to anger and depression. With regard to gender, consistent with previous studies, females experienced higher depression than males, and there is no gender difference with regard to anger (Broidy & Agnew, 1997; Broidy, 2001).

Table 4 The Relationship between all Strain Variables, Delinquency and Aggression in the U.S.[12]

Variable	Model1- Damaging property	Model2- Hitting someone	Model3- Alcohol use	Model4- Aggression
Goal strain	.003(.014)	.002(.008)	.008(.012)	.019(.014)
Unjust strain	.010(.013)	.026(.011)*	.006(.011)	.039(.013)**
Negative life-event	.026(.009)**	.017(.008)*	.021(.007)**	-.009(.009)
Victimization	.068(.013)**	.105(.011)**	.075(.012)**	.077(.014)**
Age	.016(.025)	-.034(.022)	.289(.020)**	-.099(.022)**
Male	.161(.085)	.317(.076)**	-.188(.071)**	-.446(.087)**

*p < .05. **p < .01.
[1] Unstandardized coefficients are shown with standard errors in parentheses, and the coefficients are the averaged estimation across the 5 data sets.
[2] The sample size is 1,516 for the three delinquent acts but is only 1,397 for aggression.

GST argues that strain not only leads to delinquent reactions but also generates negative feelings in the recipients, which in turn make the individual want to respond in such a way as to correct the bad feeling. Although GST does propose that strain has direct effects on delinquency, it is the indirect effect, through negative emotions, that separates GST from other leading criminological theories (e.g., control theory). Table 5 presents the results of testing the full GST model, and Table 6 provides the results of total indirect effects of a particular strain on the four outcome variables through anger and depression.

In the full model, both anger and depression have significant influences on the three delinquent acts and the effects are relatively large when compared to the effects of all strain variables. However, only anger is significantly related to aggression against siblings. As such, anger and depression are both potent candidates as mediators of strain effects on the three delinquent acts but only anger could be a mediator when the outcome is aggression (Baron & Kenny, 1986). The finding that anger is related to alcohol use is surprising because previous studies suggest that anger is most likely to lead to outer-directed delinquency, such as physical aggression (Aseltine et al., 2000; Jang & Johnson, 2005), rather than inner-directed coping strategies (e.g., substance use). In contrast, depression was related to not only inner-directed delinquency (e.g., alcohol use) but also outer-directed acts (e.g., hitting someone).

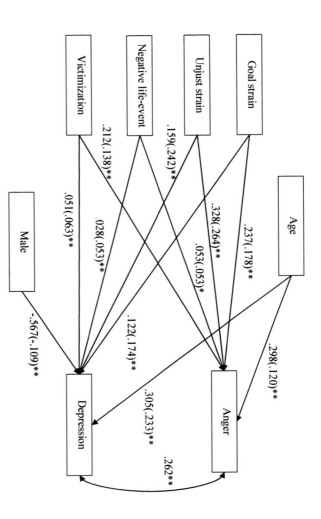

Figure 4. The Path-Analytic Model of Strain and Negative Emotions in the U.S.
Unstandardized coefficients are shown with standardized coefficients in parentheses, and the
coefficients are the averaged estimation across the 5 data sets (insignificant paths are not shown).
*p < .05. **p < .01.

Table 5 The Full GST Model in the U.S.[12]

	Model for three delinquent acts(N = 1,516)				
	Anger	Depression	Damaging property	Hitting someone	Alcohol use
Goal strain	.237(.032)**	.122(.018)**	-.021(-.014)	-.017(.013)	-.010(.012)
Unjust strain	.328(.031)**	.159(.018)**	-.023(-.013)	0(.012)	-.018(.011)
Negative life-event	.053(.023)*	.028(.012)*	.020(.009)*	.013(.008)	.017(.007)*
Victimization	.212(.036)**	.051(.019)**	.051(.012)**	.091(.011)**	.063(.012)**
Age	.298(.065)	.305(.030)**	-.027(.024)	-.068(.023)**	.255(.020)**
Male	.065(.230)**	-.567(-.122)**	.204(.083)*	.352(.075)**	-.148(.071)*
Anger			.060(.009)**	.047(.009)**	.038(.008)**
Depression			.082(.017)**	.067(.017)**	.075(.015)**

	Model for aggression (N = 1,397）		
	Anger	Depression	Aggression
Goal strain	.245(.038)**	.124(.020)**	0(.014)
Unjust strain	.322(.036)**	.159(.019)**	.013(.013)
Negative life-event	.050(.024)*	.032(.013)*	-.013(.009)
Victimization	.209(.038)**	.044(.020)*	.061(.014)**
Age	.283(.061)**	.311(.032)**	-.122(.022)**
Male	.098(.240)	-.565(.126)**	-.45(.086)**
Anger			.076(.010)**
Depression			.006(.019)

*p < .05, **p < .01.

[1] Unstandardized coefficients are shown with standard errors in parentheses, and the coefficients are the averaged estimation from the 5 complete datasets.

[2] All the models are estimated with anger being correlated with depression. The correlation is .262 when the outcome variables are the three delinquent acts and is .260 when the outcome variable is aggression.

Although these findings may not echo those of previous studies in the GST literature, results of studies from other areas have found similar results. For example, anger was found to be related to the amount of alcohol consumption and substance use (Eftekhari, Turner, & Larimer, 2004; Hussong & Chassin, 1994; Terrell, Miller, Foster, & Watkins, 2006), and even negative emotions closely related to anger, such as hostility (Hussong, Hicks, Levy & Curran, 2001), increased alcohol use.

Similarly, depression also has strong and statistically significant effects on all three delinquent acts. This finding is consistent with research by Beyers and Loeber (2003), who found that depression was related to other-directed delinquent behaviors, such as shoplifting and using force to get something. However, the present finding is surprising because previous studies in the GST literature found that depression was related to inner-directed deviant behavior, such as substance use (Jang. 2007; Jang & Johnson, 2003) or purging (Sharp et al., 2005), not outer-directed delinquency.

The most pronounced result is that victimization has statistically significant and relatively large effects on all the outcome variables and on both of the two negative emotions. This suggests that students who experience more victimization incidents are more likely to react to this stressor with delinquency and to display anger and depression. Whereas the indirect effects from victimization to the four outcome variables through anger are all significant, victimization has significant indirect effects on the three delinquencies through depression only. The indirect relationship between victimization and aggression through depression is not significant. While the indirect effects on the three delinquent acts are all significant, these indirect effects account for only 13% to

25% of the total effects (see Table 7). These results again indicate that criminal victimization, whether violent or property victimization, is a criminogenic strain (Agnew, 2006a), and most of its detrimental effect comes from the victimization itself.

Negative life-events is moderately and significantly related to property damage and alcohol use but only marginally related to hitting someone. With regard to mediating effects, negative life-events has indirect effects through anger on the four outcome variables but has such effects through depression only on the three delinquent acts . The most interesting difference between Table 4 and Table 5 is that of the negative life-event → hit someone relationship, which changes from significant to marginally significant when both anger and depression were in the model. According to Baron and Kenny (1986), this would indicate that a significant mediating effect exists. In Table 6, the indirect effects of negative life-event to hitting someone through anger (.002) and depression (.002) are all significant, although the effects are small. However, the mediating effect is only partial because the direct effect still accounts for over 70% of total effects of negative life-event to hitting someone (see Table 7).

In contrast to victimization and negative life-events, goal strain and unjust strain are related to delinquency and aggression mostly through anger and depression. The total indirect effect, for instance, of goal strain to property damage is greater than the direct effect. For unjust strain, its impact on hitting someone, for example, is mediated through anger (58%) and depression (38%).

144

Table 6 The Indirect Effects of Strains on Outcome Variables through Anger and Depression in the U.S.[123]

Variable	Damaging property[3] [2]	Hitting someone	Alcohol use	Aggression
Goal strain→Anger	.014[.008, .021][2]	.011[.006, .017]	.009[.005, .015]	.019[.011, .027]
Unjust strain→Anger	.020[.013, .028]	.016[.010, .022]	.012[.006, .018]	.025[.016, .033]
Negative life-event→Anger	.003[.007, .021]	.002[0, .005]	.002[0, .012]	.004[0, .008]
Victimization→Anger	.013[.008, .019]	.010[.006, .015]	.008[.004, .012]	.016[.009, .023]
Goal strain→Depression	.010[.006, .016]	.008[.003, .014]	.009[.005, .015]	NS[a]
Unjust strain→Depression	.013[.008, .019]	.01[.005, .015]	.012[.007, .018]	NS
Negative life-event→Depression	.003[0, .004]	.002[0, .004]	.002[0, .004]	NS
Victimization→Depression	.004[.001, .009]	.004[.001, .007]	.004[.001, .008]	NS

[1] The indirect effect reported here is the average from the 5 complete datasets.
[2] The total sample size is 1,516 for the three delinquent acts, and is 1,397 for aggression.
[3] 95% confidence interval is in the bracket.
[a] Non-significant indirect effect is not reported here.

Moreover, unjust strain has strong indirect effects on aggression against siblings through anger, which accounts for 64% of total effects (see Table 7). This latter result not only supports GST's contention regarding the mediating role of negative emotion in the GST model (Agnew, 1992, 2001) but also undergirds recent empirical evidence of the supremacy of state-like measures of negative emotion when more situational measures of negative emotions are used (Capowich et al., 2001; Mazerolle et al., 2003).

In sum, two general conclusions can be reached. First, victimization has statistically significant and relatively strong impact on students' life; that is, students who experience criminal victimization have higher probability of involvement in delinquency and aggression and these students are also more likely to experience anger and depression, which in turn leads to greater involvement in delinquency, compared with students who do not have such experience. Negative life-events, a commonly used measure of strain, also has statistically significant and moderate effects on delinquency but not on aggression. Goal strain and unjust strain, on the other hand, exert few or no direct effects on delinquency and aggression; most of the effects these two strains have on the outcome variables are through anger and depression.

Second, the proposed mediating effects of negative emotions on the strain-delinquency relationship were present. In some cases, a total mediating effect was found. For example, the unjust strain → hitting someone relationship was totally mediated by anger and depression. This result not only supports GST's assertion that negative emotion plays a causal role in crime and delinquency but also supports Agnew's (2006a, 2006b) argument that negative emotions other than anger should be included in the GST

146

model. On the other hand, both anger and depression are related to delinquency

regardless of whether it is inner-directed (e.g., alcohol use) or outer-directed delinquency

(e.g., hitting someone). This is unexpected, because GST would predict the domain

match relationship (e.g., outer-directed emotion (anger) → outer-directed coping (hitting

someone). However, studies from other areas provide some empirical support for the

mismatch results (Eftekhari et al., 2004; Beyers & Loeber, 2003; Terrell et al., 2006).

Table 7 The Direct, Indirect, and Total Effects in the U.S.

Paths	Direct effect	Indirect effect	Total effect
Goal strain → damaging property	-.021	.024	.003
Unjust strain → damaging property	-.023	.033	.010
Negative life-event → damaging property	.020	.006	.026
Victimization → damaging property	.051	.017	.068
Goal strain → hitting someone	-.017	.019	.002
Unjust strain → hitting someone	0	.026	.026
Negative life-event → hitting someone	.013	.004	.017
Victimization → hitting someone	.091	.014	.105
Goal strain → alcohol use	-.010	.018	.008
Unjust strain → alcohol use	-.018	.024	.006
Negative life-event → alcohol use	.017	.004	.021
Victimization → alcohol use	.063	.012	.075
Goal strain → aggression	0	.019	.019
Unjust strain → aggression	.013	.026[1]	.039
Negative life-event → aggression	-.013	.004	-.009
Victimization → aggression	.061	.016	.077

[1] The indirect effect is slightly greater than that in Table 5 because of the non-significant indirect effect through depression.

GST in Taiwan

The above analyses show that the GST model is useful in explaining juvenile delinquency and aggression in the U.S. This is understandable because the origins of GST, the classic strain theory, and GST itself were developed in the U.S. As reviewed in Chapter III, the cultural background of the U.S. is different from that of Taiwan. This may raise the question of whether GST is extendable to non-western countries, such as Taiwan. This section directly addresses this issue by using the data derived from the same survey instrument, similar subjects, and identical statistical and theoretical models. In addition, this can be considered as a replication of the U.S. study, which according to Robinson and Levin (1997, p.26), is valuable in that it can not only "confirm previous findings but also extend those findings to new possibility." This is especially true in the present study because the replication is done by samples from different culture.

We first investigated whether the same four strain variables used in the U.S. analysis have any effects on the three delinquent acts and on aggression. Table 8 provides the results of this inquiry. Although goal strain and unjust strain have statistically significant effects on delinquent acts, the effects are relatively small. In contrast, negative life-events and victimization are statistically significant and strong predictors of delinquency and of aggression. These results confirmed what was found in the U.S. sample that victimization and negative life-events are crimnogenic.

Negative emotion plays an important role in GST; in fact, GST argues that strain makes an individual feel bad, i.e., strain engenders negative emotions. The next step is to test whether this argument holds in Taiwan. Figure 5 presents this test.

148

Table 8 The Relationship between all Strain Variables, Delinquency and Aggression in
Taiwan[1]

Variable	Model1-Damaging property[2]	Model2-Hitting someone	Model3-Alcohol use	Model4-Aggression
Goal strain	.024(.011)*	.008(.012)	.006(.009)	.030(.009)**
Unjust strain	.025(.011)*	.031(.011)**	.019(.009)*	.007(.009)
Negative life-event	.030(.007)**	.039(.008)*	.027(.006)**	.016(.006)**
Victimization	.031(.009)**	.034(.010)**	.013(.009)	.032(.010)**
Age	.004(.027)	-.066(.032)*	.061(.021)**	-.144(.020)**
Male	.445(.085)**	.403(.100)**	.039(.066)	.071(.065)

$*p < .05.$ $**p <. 01.$
[1] Unstandardized coefficients are shown with standard errors in parentheses, and the
coefficients are the averaged estimation across the 5 data sets.
[2]The sample size for the three delinquent acts is 1,717 but is only 1,610 for aggression.

As can be seen, the relationships between the four strain variables and anger and

depression are all significant. Among all the strain variables, goal strain and unjust strain

have strong and statistically significant effects on depression and anger. This is consistent

with the results found in the U.S. sample. One noticeable finding is that gender does not

have a significant and negative effect on depression. Previous studies have shown that

females usually experience and report higher levels of depression than do males

(Mirowsky & Ross, 1995; Sharp et al., 2005). However, as explained in a previous

chapter, Chinese people are more likely to identify somatic problems rather than

psychological ones. Consequently, a gender difference could be wiped out because of this

tendency.

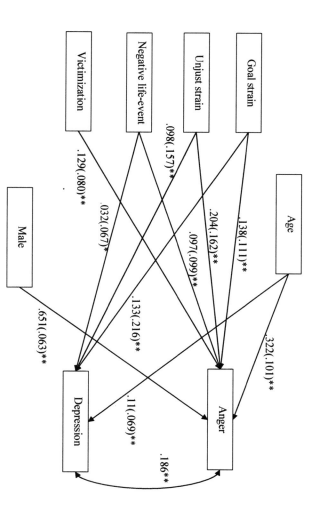

Figure 5. The Path-Analytic Model of Strain and Negative Emotions in Taiwan: Unstandardized coefficients are shown with standardized coefficients in parentheses, and the coefficients are the averaged estimation across the 5 data sets (insignificant paths are not shown).
*p < .05. **p < .01.

Also, male students report a higher level of anger than do female students. Although Broidy and Agnew (1997) argue that females may experience a higher level of anger than males, a study from Singapore showed that women from a Chinese culture, which is patriarchal and places high priority on relational harmony, hesitated to reveal their anger (Tanzer, Sim, & Spielberger, 1996). Consequently, female students may tend to underreport their anger more than male students do.

The above two models show that students in Taiwan who experience strain are more likely not only to experience anger and depression but also to be involved in delinquency and aggression. However, these tests were performed only to build the foundation for further examination of the full GST model, in which all variables are incorporated in one model simultaneously. Table 9 provides the results of testing the full GST model. Anger and depression mediate most of the relationships between goal strain, unjust strain, and outcome variables (see Table 10).

More dramatically, anger and depression have totally mediated the goal strain-hitting someone relationship; that is, the effects that goal strain have on hitting someone is through anger and depression. Similarly, unjust strain also lost its influence on damaging property and alcohol use. The indirect effect, for instance, from this strain through anger to alcohol use is .004 and .006 through depression. The total indirect effects account for about 53% of the total effects of unjust strain on alcohol use (see Table 11). This indicates that most of the negative influence of unjust strain on youths is through its instigation of anger and depression.

151

Table 9 The Full GST Model in Taiwan[12]

	Model for three delinquent acts (N = 1,717)				
	Anger	Depression	Damaging property	Hitting someone	Alcohol use
Goal strain	.138(.025)**	.133(.014)**		-.003(.012)	-.005(.009)
Unjust strain	.204(.027)**	.098(.015)**	.014(.011)	.019(.011)	.009(.009)
Negative life-event	.097(.020)*	.032(.012)**	.026(.007)**	.033(.008)**	.023(.006)**
Victimization	.129(.026)**	.035(.017)*	.026(.009)**	.027(.010)**	.008(.009)
Age	.322(.080)**	.110(.036)**	-.010(.027)	-.084(.032)**	-.047(.021)*
Male	.652(.242)**	-.143(-.118)	.432(.085)**	.381(.099)**	.033(.066)
Anger			.029(.008)**	.043(.009)**	.022(.006)**
Depression			.046(.016)**	.037(.017)*	.059(.013)**

	Model for aggression (N = 1,611)		
	Anger	Depression	Aggression
Goal strain	.121(.032)**	.128(.016)**	.024(.009)**
Unjust strain	.201(.032)**	.096(.016)**	-.001(.009)
Negative life-event	.099(.024)**	.030(.011)*	.013(.006)*
Victimization	.140(.039)**	.037(.019)	.027(.01)**
Age	.339(.077)**	.119(.037)**	-.157(.020)**
Male	.654(.248)**	-.148(.121)	.052(.065)**
Anger			.033(.007)**
Depression			.015(.014)

*p < .05. **p < .01.

[1] Unstandardized coefficients are shown with standard errors in parentheses, and the coefficients are the averaged estimation from the 5 complete datasets.

[2] All the models are estimated with anger being correlated with depression. The correlation is .186 when the outcome variables are the delinquent acts and is .177 when the outcome variable is aggression.

Table 10 The Indirect Effects of Strains on Outcome Variables through Anger and Depression in Taiwan[1]

Variable	Damaging property[2]	Hitting someone	Alcohol use	Aggression
Goal strain→Anger	.004[.001, .008][3]	.006[.002, .011]	.003[.001, .006]	.004[.001, .008]
Unjust strain→Anger	.006[.003, .009]	.009[.005, .014]	.004[.002, .008]	.007[.003, .011]
Negative life-event→Anger	.003[.001, .005]	.004[.002, .007]	.002[.001, .014]	.003[.001, .006]
Victimization→Anger	.004[.001, .008]	.006[.001, .012]	.003[0, .007]	.005[.001, .010]
Goal strain→Depression	.006[.001, .011]	.005[0, .010][a]	.008[.004, .013]	NS[a]
Unjust strain→Depression	.005[.001, .008]	.003[0, .008][a]	.006[.003, .009]	NS
Negative life-event→Depression	.001[0, .003]	.002[0, .003]	.002[.001, .003]	NS
Victimization→Depression	.001[0, .004]	.001[0, .004]	.002[0, .005]	NS

[1] The indirect effect reported here is the average from the 5 complete datasets.
[2] The total sample size is 1,717for the three delinquent acts, and is 1,611 for aggression.
[3] 95% confidence interval is in the bracket.
[a] NS: Non-significant at .05 and .1 level.

This indicates that most of the negative influence of unjust strain on youths is through its instigation of anger and depression. This result reveals the importance of examining the full GST model; leaving out negative emotions may provide only a partial picture of the complex relationships between strain and delinquency in the adolescent year.

Negative life-events continually exert significant effects on all the outcome variables. This is consistent with much previous research, whether the study was conducted in western or eastern countries (Aseltine & Gore, 2000; Eitle & Turner, 2003; Lin, in press; Lin & Mieczkowski, 2011). However, the indirect effects account only for 13% to 19% of the total effects of negative life-event on all the outcome variables. Consequently, negative life-events are detrimental to youths primarily because of direct effects.

Victimization, like negative life-events, has significant effects on delinquency and aggression but not on alcohol use. As in the case of negative life-events, the most negative influence comes from the victimization experience itself, because the indirect effects account only for 14% to 20% of all the effects. The only exception is that anger and depression have strong mediating effects on alcohol use. The indirect effect accounts for about 38% of the total effect. Similar to the results with the U.S. sample, victimization, measured in the present study, is detrimental to youths in Taiwan; and a similar result was found in one previous study, which used a random sample of Taiwanese adolescents (Lin & Mieczkowski, 2011).

Table 11 The Direct, Indirect, and Total Effects in Taiwan

Paths	Direct effect	Indirect effect	Total effect
Goal strain → damaging property	.014	.010	.024
Unjust strain → damaging property	.014	.011	.025
Negative life-event → damaging property	.026	.004	.030
Victimization → damaging property	.026	.005	.031
Goal strain → hitting someone	-.003	.011	.008
Unjust strain → hitting someone	.019	.012	.031
Negative life-event → hitting someone	.033	.006	.039
Victimization → hitting someone	.027	.007	.034
Goal strain → alcohol use	-.005	.011	.006
Unjust strain → alcohol use	.009	.010	.019
Negative life-event → alcohol use	.023	.004	.027
Victimization → alcohol use	.008	.005	.013
Goal strain → aggression	.024	.006[1]	.030
Unjust strain → aggression	-.001	.008[1]	.007
Negative life-event → aggression	.013	.003	.016
Victimization → aggression	.027	.005	.032

[1] The indirect effect is slightly greater than that in Table 5 because of the non-significant indirect effect through depression.

In sum, the results of the analysis in Taiwan generally support GST. First, negative life-events and victimization have statistically significant and large direct effects on delinquency and aggression. These two strains also have statistically significant effects on anger and depression. As in the U.S., victimization and negative life-events are detrimental to youths not only because of the strain itself but also through the negative emotions—anger and depression—that ensue. However, the indirect effects account only for 10 to 20 percent of total effects. Hence, the most negative influence of these two strains on adolescents lies in the strain itself, a conclusion consistent with results of previous studies that found that negative life-events and victimization both have effects on delinquency and aggression.

Second, although goal strain and unjust strain have various direct effects on delinquency and aggression, in the full GST model, anger and depression mediate most of their effects on the four outcome variables. The most significant change is that the influences of goal strain on hitting someone and alcohol use are reduced to almost 0 but the effects on hitting someone and alcohol use are taken up by anger and depression. This same result is also found in the unjust strain-aggression relationship; in addition, anger and depression totally mediated the strain-delinquency relationship.

Multiple group analysis

The final analysis provides the statistical basis for comparing the GST model across the U.S. and Taiwan. As mentioned in the previous chapter, multiple group analysis is preferable to other methods with regard to comparing path models across different populations. Multiple group analysis is not only capable of discovering similarities (e.g., imposing equality on a parameter) but also suitable for revealing differences (e.g., freeing a parameter). The present study uses a step-up approach[41] to conduct the multiple group analysis; that is, the GST model is free to be estimated for each group and then restrictions on a path are imposed one by one. Imposing a constraint on a path frees a degree of freedom; if the chi-square difference is not over 3.84, the path is said to be the same across countries. In contrast, if the chi-square difference is greater than 3.84, the constrained path is said to be different[42]. A model with more degrees of freedom is more parsimonious than a model with fewer degrees of freedom if both

[41] In contrast to a step-down approach, a researcher starts with the most restricted model, and subsequent models are evaluated by sequentially relaxing the constraints.

[42] The chi-square is not directly useable for the chi-square difference testing because the estimator is not ML but WLSMV. Fortunately, Mplus provides syntax (DIFFTEST) to fulfill this task.

models fit the data similarly. Hence, a parsimonious model is preferred to a complex model with similar fit.

The restrictions that are enforced are based on the results of separated analyses because the empirically found similarities and differences can be further tested. Before any restrictions are imposed, the least restricted model, or the most complex model (e.g., all paths are free to be estimated) was tested. The results can be found in Table 12 and Table 13. As can be seen, unjust strain and goal strain have no direct effects on delinquency in both samples. Similarly, negative life-event and victimization continue to exert statistically significant and large direct effects on delinquency and aggression in both countries. The only exception is that in the U.S., negative life-events does not have a significant effect on aggression, which is not the case in Taiwan. In addition, anger and depression remain potent risk factors in delinquency in both countries, but only anger increases the risk of involvement in aggression in both U.S. and Taiwan.

Table 12 The Full GST Model-Multiple Group Analysis for Delinquent Acts[123]

	Anger	Depression	Damaging property	Hitting someone	Alcohol use
Model for the U.S. (N = 1,516)					
Goal strain	.237(.032)**	.122(.018)**	-.021(.014)	-.017(.013)	-.010(.012)
Unjust strain	.328(.031)**	.159(.018)**	-.023(.013)	0(.012)	-.018(.011)
Negative life-event	.053(.023)*	.028(.012)*	.020(.009)*	.013(.008)	.017(.007)*
Victimization	.211(.036)**	.051(.019)**	.051(.012)**	.091(.011)**	.063(.012)**
Age	.298(.080)**	.305(.030)**	-.027(.024)	-.068(.023)**	.255(.02)**
Gender	.066(.242)	-.567(.122)**	.204(.083)*	.352(.075)**	-.148(.071)*
Anger			.060(.009)**	.047(.009)**	.038(.008)**
Depression			.082(.017)**	.067(.017)**	.075(.015)**
Model for Taiwan (N = 1,717)					
Goal strain	.138(.025)**	.133(.014)**	.014(.011)	-.003(.012)	-.005(.009)
Unjust strain	.204(.027)**	.098(.015)**	.014(.011)	.019(.011)	.009(.009)
Negative life-event	.097(.02)**	.032(.012)*	.026(.007)**	.033(.008)**	.023(.006)**
Victimization	.129(.026)**	.035(.017)*	.026(.009)**	.027(.010)**	.008(.009)
Age	.322(.080)**	.110(.036)**	-.010(.020)	-.084(.032)**	.047(.021)*
Gender	.651(.242)**	-.143(.118)	.432(.085)**	.381(.099)**	.033(.066)
Anger			.029(.008)**	.043(.009)**	.022(.006)**
Depression			.046(.016)**	.037(.017)*	.059(.013)**

*p < .05. **p < .01.

[1] Unstandardized coefficients are shown, with standard errors in parentheses, and the coefficients are the averaged estimation from the 5 complete datasets.

[2] All path are free to be estimated.

[3] Model is estimated with anger correlated with depression (r = .262-U.S.; r = .186-Taiwan).

158

Table 13 The Full GST Model-Multiple Group Analysis for Aggression[123]

	Anger	Depression	Aggression
Model for the U.S. (N = 1,397)			
Goal strain	.245(.038)**	.124(.020)**	0(.014)
Unjust strain	.322(.036)**	.159(.019)**	.013(.013)
Negative life-event	.050(.024)*	.032(.013)*	-.013(.009)
Victimization	.209(.038)**	.044(.02)*	.061(.014)**
Age	.283(.061)**	.311(.032)**	-.123(.022)**
Gender	.098(.240)	-.565(.126)**	-.045(.085)**
Anger			.077(.010)**
Depression			.004(.019)
Model for Taiwan (N = 1,611)			
Goal strain	.121(.032)**	.128(.016)**	.024(.009)**
Unjust strain	.201(.032)**	.096(.016)**	0(.009)
Negative life-event	.099(.024)**	.030(.011)**	.013(.006)*
Victimization	.140(.039)**	.037(.019)	.027(.010)**
Age	.339(.077)**	.119(.037)**	-.157(.020)**
Gender	.654(.248)**	-.148(.121)	.053(.065)
Anger			.033(.007)**
Depression			.015(.014)

*p < .05. **p <. 01.
[1]Unstandardized coefficients are shown, with standard errors in parentheses, and the coefficients are the averaged estimation from the 5 complete datasets.
[2]All path are free to be estimated.
[3]Model is estimated with anger correlated with depression (r = .260-U.S.; r = .177-Taiwan).

All these results indicate that if we stop here, the conclusion is that the GST model is reasonably similar across cultural boundaries. This conclusion is important, because the data were collected on the basis of almost identical survey items and because the multiple group analysis allows direct comparison across populations. This conclusion confirms that of previous studies that only indirectly compared results across countries (Bao et al., 2004; Lin & Mieczkowski, 2011; Maxwell, 2001; Moon & Morash, 2004). However, more can be gained if the differences of path coefficients are directly examined.

The results from Table 12 and 13 provide the basis for imposing constraints on paths. The most interesting differences[43] related to damaging property are: goal strain → damaging property, unjust strain → damaging property, and negative life-event → damaging property. In addition, although the effects of strains on anger and depression are all significant for both countries, the magnitude differs and studies have suggested that cultural influences affect the expression of negative emotions. As such, imposing constraints on the strain-negative emotions paths are also warranted.

Table 14 provides a summary of the results of the constraints imposed on paths as outlined above. As can be seen, students who experienced negative life-events are more likely to experience depression and anger in both the U.S. and Taiwan, and the magnitude is the same for these strain-negative emotion relationships. On the other hand, students who experience victimization are more likely to experience similar magnitude of depression in both countries than students who do not have the experience. The same applied to the goal strain-depression relationship. However, while unjust strain and goal strain both increase students' anger, the magnitude is not the same across countries. The magnitude is always stronger in the U.S. than is it in Taiwan.

---

[43] Three criteria are used to impose constraints on a path: a path is significant in one country but not in another country, the sign of the path is different across countries, or the difference of the magnitude of the path is dramatically different across countries.

160

Table 14 The Full GST Model-Multiple Group Analysis with Constraints (Damaging Property)[1,2,3]

	Anger		Depression		Damaging property	
	U.S.	Taiwan	U.S.	Taiwan	U.S.	Taiwan
Goal strain	.230(.032)**	.140(.025)**	.129(.011)**		.001(.005)	
Unjust strain	.328(.031)**	.204(.027)**	.159(.018)**	.098(.015)**	-.022(.013)	.014(.011)
Negative life-event	.077(.015)*		.030(.009)**	.023(.005)**		
Victimization	.211(.036)**	.129(.011)**	.042(.013)**		.052(.013)**	.025(.009)**
Age	.298(.059)**	.322(.080)**	.305(.030)**		-.011(.027)	-.025(.024)
Gender	.066(.230)	.651(.242)**	.111(.036)**	.202(.083)**	.432(.085)**	-.011(.027)
Anger			-.567(.122)**	-.143(.118)	.030(.008)**	.058(.009)**
Depression					.049(.016)**	.079(.017)**

*p < .05. **p < .01.

[1] Unstandardized coefficients are shown, with standard errors in parentheses, and the coefficients are the averaged estimation from the 5 complete datasets (N = 1,516-U.S.; N = 1,717-Taiwan).

[2] Model is estimated with anger correlated with depression (r = .268-U.S.; r = .185-Taiwan).

[3] The model fits the data well: $\chi^2(6) = 7.21$, NS; CFI = .999; TLI = .992; RMSEA = .011

Table 15 The Full GST Model-Multiple Group Analysis with Constraints (Hitting Someone)[123]

	Anger		Depression		Hitting Someone	
	U.S.	Taiwan	U.S.	Taiwan	U.S.	Taiwan
Goal strain	.237(.033)**	.138(.025)**	.129(.011)**		-.017(.013)	-.003(.012)
Unjust strain	.325(.031)**	.207(.028)**	.157(.018)**	.098(.015)**	.010(.008)	
Negative life-event	.077(.015)**		.030(.008)**		.023(.005)**	
Victimization	.211(.036)**	.129(.026)**	.042(.013)*		.092(.011)**	.027(.010)**
Age	.298(.059)**	.323(.080)**	.305(.030)**	.110(.036)**	-.067(.023)**	-.084(.032)**
Gender	.064(.230)	.651(.242)**	-.567(.122)**	-.143(.118)	.351(.075)**	.380(.099)**
Anger					.045(.006)**	.039(.017)*
Depression					.065(.017)**	

*p < .05. **p < .01.

[1] Unstandardized coefficients are shown, with standard errors in parentheses, and the coefficients are the averaged estimation from the 5 complete datasets (N = 1,516-U.S.; N = 1,717-Taiwan).

[2] Model is estimated with anger correlated with depression (r = .263-U.S.; r = .186-Taiwan).

[3] The model fits the data well: $\chi^2(7) = 8.37$, NS; CFI =.999; TLI = .993; RMSEA = .011

As reviewed in previous chapters, maintaining relational harmony is of high priority in a collectivistic culture; in addition, the Confucian ethos regards the expression of anger as immature. Therefore, the stronger effects may be attributed to the reluctance of Chinese students to express anger, especially when the source of anger is goal-related or relationship-related. When looking at results related to depression, the only cultural difference is seen in the unjust strain-depression relationship, with this relationship being stronger in the U.S. sample. The other three strain-depression relationships are similar across the U.S. and Taiwan.

With regard to the three paths on which constraints were imposed, only one, unjust strain → damaging property, was rejected ($\chi^2(1) = 5.44$, p<.05). Although the magnitude and the sign of this path are different for the U.S. and Taiwan, the path has an insignificant effect on damaging property in both countries. The other three imposed constraints did not make the model fit worse; hence, goal strain does not have any influence on damaging property in either country, whereas negative life-events exerts a significant effect on damaging property in both countries, with the same magnitude. Victimization, anger, and depression continue to have effects on damaging property in both countries, although the magnitude of effects is different and is always stronger in the U.S. than in Taiwan.

With regard to hitting someone, in addition to the imposed constraints on the strain-negative emotion relationship, 4 other constraints were imposed: unjust strain → hitting someone, negative life-events → hitting someone, victimization → hitting someone, and anger → hitting someone. As shown in Table 15, the strain-negative

163

emotion relationships were all similar to those of Table 14. Of the four additional imposed constraints, one was rejected (victimization → hitting someone) ($\chi^2(1) = 21.78$, p<.01). Hence, although victimization is a risk factor for violent delinquency (e.g., hitting someone) in both countries, the effect of this stressor on hitting someone is significantly stronger in the U.S. than in Taiwan.

Negative life-events is also an important risk factor for hitting someone in both countries, but the influence is about the same. The most interesting similarity is that of the anger-hitting someone relationship, because one would expect to see that this relationship is stronger in the U.S. than in Taiwan. However, the imposed constraint does not make model fit worse, which indicates that the relationship is the same across cultures. This is surprising, because one would expect that Chinese students would have lower levels of anger, which in turn leads to a lower incidence of violent acts. One possible counter explanation is the recent surge of violent crime and campus violence in Taiwan, as reviewed in Chapter III, which might make students more likely to vent anger through violent acts. Moreover, what we discover here is the anger-hitting someone relationship, which indicates that angered students are more likely to be involved in violent delinquency but does not mean that students are equally angry or equally violent in the two countries[44].

---

[44] The t-test showed that the U.S. students have significantly higher levels of anger than do Taiwanese students (t = 10.1, p < .01). The proportion of students in Taiwan who report yes on hitting someone is only 7%, whereas the proportion for the U.S. is 24%.

164

In Table 16, five paths deserve particular attention: goal strain → alcohol use, unjust strain → alcohol use, victimization → alcohol use, anger → alcohol use, and depression → alcohol use. The constraints on these four paths and those imposed on the strain-negative emotions path are examined. The results (Table 16) are fairly similar to those found in Table 14 and 15 insofar as strain-negative emotion is concerned. Of the five listed paths, only one was rejected: victimization → alcohol use ($\chi^2(1) = 14.93$, p < .01). Hence, victimization has dramatically different effects on alcohol use in both countries. On the one hand, students in the U.S. drink alcohol to cope with victimization; on the other hand, students in Taiwan do not employ such a coping strategy. This is somewhat unexpected, but two explanations can be offered. In Taiwan, students are under close supervision by family members and others because of the small land area and crowding. Hence, opportunities for deviant behavior are greatly reduced. Another possibility is that the drinking norms in the Chinese culture demand that individuals drink with others or during feasts or meal time (Harrell, 1981). Students in Taiwan may be aware of this norm, and may reject alcohol use as a coping strategy.

Other imposed paths do not make the model fit worse. As a result, the similarities of the four paths are statistically confirmed. Hence, students in both countries who experience anger and depression are more likely to use alcohol. However, it also shows that goal strain and unjust strain have no effects on drinking alcohol in either the U.S. or Taiwan. In contrast, negative life-events exerts a significant effect on alcohol use in both countries, but the magnitude differs significantly.

165

Table 16 The Full GST Model-Multiple Group Analysis with Constraints (Alcohol Use)[1][2][3]

	Anger		Depression		Alcohol Use	
	U.S.	Taiwan	U.S.	Taiwan	U.S.	Taiwan
Goal strain	.237(.033)**	.138(.025)**	.129(.011)**		-.007(.007)	
Unjust strain	.325(.031)**	.207(.027)**	.157(.018)**	.099(.015)**	-.001(.007)	
Negative life-event		.077(.015)**				
Victimization	.212(.036)**	.129(.026)**	.030(.008)**		.017(.007)*	.023(.006)**
Age	.298(.059)**	.322(.080)**	.042(.013)*		.066(.012)**	.007(.009)
Gender	.065(.230)	.651(.242)**	.306(.030)**	.110(.036)**	.260(.020)**	.044(.021)*
Anger			-.567(.122)**	-.143(.118)	-.152(.070)*	.030(.066)
Depression					.029(.005)**	.067(.010)**

*p < .05. **p < .01.

[1] Unstandardized coefficients are shown, with standard errors in parentheses, and the coefficients are the averaged estimation from the 5 complete datasets (N = 1,516-U.S.; N = 1,717-Taiwan).

[2] Model is estimated with anger correlated with depression (r = .263-U.S.; r = .186-Taiwan).

[3] The model fits the data well: $\chi^2(8)$ = 9.31, NS; CFI =.999; TLI = .995; RMSEA = 0

166

With regard to aggression (Table 17), constraints are imposed on four paths: goal strain → aggression, unjust strain → aggression, negative life-events → aggression, and victimization → aggression, in addition to the constraints imposed on strain-negative emotions. Among all these imposed constraints, the latter two paths are rejected: negative life-event → aggression ($\chi^2(1) = 6.06$, p<.05) and victimization → aggression ($\chi^2(1) = 3.85$, p<.05). Consequently, these two paths were seen to be different across countries. The most dramatic change is the goal strain-aggression relationship, which becomes significant in the U.S., although it was not significant before. Hence, goal strain and victimization are related to aggression in both countries. Anger exerts significant effects on aggression, which is consistent with GST's prediction; however, the magnitude is different across countries, with a stronger effect in the U.S. sample. Similarly, depression has no effects on aggression in either the U.S. or Taiwan

So far, the comparison has focused on the direct relationships between strain, negative emotions, and outcome variables. Another important part of GST is consideration of the indirect effect of strain on delinquency through negative emotions. To examine whether a particular indirect effect is statistically different between the U.S. and Taiwan, the Wald statistic is used[45]. The Wald statistic can be used to test the specified parameter(s) all at once; that is, we can test all the indirect effects simultaneously. However, it gives only the overall result (e.g., all the indirect effects are the same).

---

[45] The Wald statistic is compared against the Chi-square distribution. The number of the degrees of freedom is based on the number of parameters tested in the hypothesis.

Table 17 The Full GST Model-Multiple Group Analysis with Constraints (Aggression)[1][2][3]

	Anger		Depression		Aggression	
	U.S.	Taiwan	U.S.	Taiwan	U.S.	Taiwan
Goal strain	.249(.037)**	.121(.032)**	.126(.012)**		.017(.007)*	
Unjust strain	.319(.035)**	.2(.032)**	.158(.017)**	.097(.015)**		.003(.007)
Negative life-event	.075(.017)**		.031(.009)**		-.013(.009)	.013(.006)*
Victimization	.175(.027)**		.04(.014)**		.059(.014)**	.027(.010)**
Age	.276(.061)**	.33(.076)**	.31(.032)**	.119(.037)**	-.118(.022)**	-.156(.02)**
Gender	.129(.239)	.613(.247)*	-.565(.125)**	-.149(.12)	-.47(.085)**	.059(.065)
Anger					.076(.010)**	.033(.007)**
Depression					.002(.018)	.017(.013)

*p < .05. **p < .01.

[1] Unstandardized coefficients are shown, with standard errors in parentheses, and the coefficients are the averaged estimation from the 5 complete datasets (N = 1,397-U.S.; N = 1,611-Taiwan).

[2] Model is estimated with anger correlated with depression (r = .26-U.S.; r = .177-Taiwan).

[3] The model fits the data well: $\chi^2(7) = 5.51$, NS; CFI = 1; TLI = 1; RMSEA = 0

Hence, whether a particular indirect effect is statistically different between the U.S. and Taiwan needs to be examined separately. The study used the Wald statistic to test all at once indirect effects of the four strains, mediated by anger and depression, for each outcome variable[46]. If the result is insignificant, no further individual test is performed. In contrast, if the result turns out to be significant, an individual Wald test is conducted to find out which of these indirect paths is significant.

Table 18 provides the results of the Wald statistic tests, including overall and individual tests. As can be seen, the overall tests showed the consistent picture that the indirect effects from strains through anger on delinquency and aggression were all statistically different between the U.S. and the Taiwan. The indirect path through depression on damaging property was the only one that differed across these two nations. Close inspection of the significant overall tests provided a clear picture of the significant group differences. For example, the indirect effect of negative life-events on aggression through anger is not statistically different between the U.S. and Taiwan; however, the indirect paths from the other three types of strain to aggression through anger are statistically different.

Combining this particular result with those of Table 6 and Table 10, we discovered that the goal strain → anger → aggression process was stronger in the U.S., for instance, than it was in Taiwan because the Wald test was significant and the indirect effect was .019 in the U.S. and .004 in the Taiwan, a difference of over 4.5 times. Another example from Table 18 is that the overall test for strains → depression →

---

[46] As reported above, depression does not have a significant mediating effect on the strain-aggression relationship. Hence, no Wald test is conducted for this indirect effect.

damaging property is significant but only unjust strain → depression → damaging

property is significant. When one looks at both Table 5 and Table 9, the indirect path

from unjust strain through depression to damage is seen to be twice as great in the U.S.

(.013) as in Taiwan (.005). Hence, students in both countries might experience depression

because of unjust strain but more students in the U.S. than in Taiwan cope with

depression by damaging property.

Table 18 The Wald test for Indirect Effect

Overall test	χ^2 result
Strains→anger→damaging property	$\chi^2(4) = 18.01**$
Strains→depression→damaging property	$\chi^2(4) = 10.67*$
Strains→anger→hitting someone	$\chi^2(4) = 8.03\dagger$
Strains→depression→hitting someone	$\chi^2(4) = 7.2$
Strains→anger→alcohol use	$\chi^2(4) = 9.91*$
Strains→depression→alcohol use	$\chi^2(4) = 4.94$
Strains→anger→aggression	$\chi^2(4) = 25.61**$
Individual test	χ^2 result
Goal strain→anger→damaging property	$\chi^2(1) = 10.62**$
Unjust strain→anger→damaging property	$\chi^2(1) = 12.52**$
Victimization→anger→damaging property	$\chi^2(1) = 7.8**$
Unjust strain→depression→damaging property	$\chi^2(1) = 5.79*$
Goal strain→anger→hitting someone	$\chi^2(1) = 2.89\dagger$
Unjust strain→anger→hitting someone	$\chi^2(1) = 2.93\dagger$
Goal strain→anger→alcohol use	$\chi^2(1) = 5.63**$
Unjust strain→anger→alcohol use	$\chi^2(1) = 6.06*$
Victimization→anger→alcohol use	$\chi^2(1) = 4.5*$
Goal strain→anger→aggression	$\chi^2(1) = 13.71**$
Unjust strain→anger→aggression	$\chi^2(1) = 16.08**$
Victimization→anger→aggression	$\chi^2(1) = 8.45**$

$\dagger p < .1, *p < .05, **p < .01$

In sum, the multiple group analysis provided a deeper understanding of the GST

model in both countries. Some cultural differences were discovered, whether in the direct

or indirect effects. Generally, the strains used in the present study engendered depression

170

in students in both countries; in contrast, students in the U.S. were more likely than students in Taiwan to respond to strain with anger. On the other hand, students in both countries responded to negative life-events with similar levels of anger.

With regard to delinquency and aggression, victimization seemed to increase students' involvement in delinquency and aggression in both countries, but the effects were different, being stronger in the U.S. than in Taiwan. Goal strain and unjust strain had similar non-significant effects on delinquency and aggression in both countries in most cases. Negative life-events had similar and significant effects on hitting someone and damaging property, but this same strain exerted different effects on alcohol use and aggression in either country.

The final tests of indirect effects provided even closer examination of the GST process. The general pattern was that students in the U.S. were more likely than Taiwanese students to commit delinquent acts and aggression because of strain and anger. On the other hand, the indirect effects of strains on outcome variables through depression were very similar across countries. The only exception was that students in the U.S. who experienced unjust strain, which caused depressive feelings, were more likely than their counterparts in Taiwan to cope with the emotion by damaging property.

CHAPTER VII

CONCLUSION AND DISCUSSION

The present study set out to exam the GST model in both the U.S. and Taiwan.

The major purposes were: whether the GST model was useful in explaining juvenile

delinquency in both countries and whether the GST processes were different in the two

countries. It is worth mentioning that this study directly compares the GST model in two

countries that have very different cultural backgrounds. In addition, this study used

stringent statistical methods to test the mediating effects of negative emotions in the GST.

Thus, the results of this study provide great insight into the issue of applying

criminological theory in a cultural setting other than that of Western countries. As

outlined in Chapter IV, this study attempted to answer six research questions. The first

and second questions were to determine whether the basic GST model could be utilized

in the U.S. and Taiwan, that is, whether strain affected delinquency and negative

emotions in both countries. The third and fourth questions asked whether anger and

depression, the two negative emotions examined in this study, mediated the strain-

delinquency relationship in both countries. The final two research questions were mainly

concerned with the similarities and differences of the GST processes in the U.S. and

Taiwanese samples. In order to answer these research questions, two sets of data

collected in the two countries by use of identical survey instruments, were examined by path analysis, a statistical tool particularly useful in testing theoretical causal models and indirect effects across different populations. This chapter provides a summary of the major findings of the statistical analysis and discusses these findings.

<u>Summary of findings</u>

The findings of the present study can be divided into three parts: the GST model in the U.S. sample, the GST model in the Taiwanese sample, and the multiple group analysis of the GST model.

First, the study found that the basic GST model was useful in explaining juvenile delinquency and aggression in both the U.S. and Taiwan. The results show that negative life-events and victimization are detrimental to youngsters in both countries, not only because they increase youthful delinquency involvement but also because they cause high levels of depression and anger in students. In addition, victimization has positive effects on aggression in both countries (see Table 19). These findings are consistent with those of previous studies that found that victimization and negative life-events are criminogenic to youth (Carson et al., 2010; Eitle & Turner 2002; Harrell 2007; Hay & Evans 2006; Lin et al., 2011). However, victimization failed to have an effect on alcohol use in the Taiwanese sample.

In contrast to these supportive results, goal strain, as measured in the present study, did not have a statistically significant effect on any of the outcome variables in the U.S. (see Table 19). However, goal strain did have impacts on Taiwanese students' delinquent behavior, although the magnitude of the effect is not large when compared to

173

victimization and negative life-events. Whereas unjust strain had significant effects on hitting someone and on aggression in the U.S. sample, the same strain increased students' involvement in damaging property and alcohol use in the Taiwanese sample. One reason for this different cultural response pattern might be due to the collectivistic nature of Chinese culture, which as mentioned earlier, emphasizes relational harmony. As such, Taiwanese students might prefer less violent coping behavior (e.g., drinking alcohol) to more violent coping strategies (e.g., hitting someone). One might argue that damaging property is also a "violent" behavior. However, damaging property was measured in a sense more closely related to vandalism, where the owner of the property is not present. Hence, Taiwanese students may be willing to engage in this form of destructive behavior.

A consistent finding from the basic model analysis was that all the strains had positive and significant effects on depression and anger in both the U.S. and Taiwan (see Table 18). However, only victimization and negative life-events have both statistically and practically significant effects on delinquency and aggression. Consequently, although the results may be consistent with previous studies in the U.S. (Broidy 2001; De Coster & Kort-Butler, 2006; Olweus 1994; Vaux & Ruggiero, 1983) or in Asia (Moon et al., 2008; Lin, in press; Lee & Larson, 2000), the practical meaning of the findings may be limited.

Second, to answer the question of whether anger and depression mediate the strain-delinquency relationship, the study examined the full GST model, which incorporated strain, anger, depression, and outcome variables simultaneously in a path model, in the U.S. and Taiwan.

174

Table 19 Summary for the Basic GST model in the U.S. and Taiwan

Variable	Goal strain		Unjust strain		Negative life-event		Victimization	
	U.S.	Taiwan	U.S.	Taiwan	U.S.	Taiwan	U.S.	Taiwan
Damaging property	+NS	+*	+NS	+*	+**	+**	+**	+**
Hitting someone	+NS	+**	+*	+NS	+*	+*	+**	+**
Alcohol use	+NS	+NS	+NS	+*	+**	+**	+**	+NS
Aggression	+NS	+**	+*	+NS	-NS	+**	+**	+**
Anger	+**	+**	+**	+**	+**	+**	+**	+**
Depression	+**	+**	+**	+**	+**	+*	+**	+NS

+ = positive effect. - = negative effect.
NS = non-significant. * = significant at .05 level. ** = significant at .01 level.

In addition, bootstrapping was employed to investigate properly the indirect effects. Table 20, a summary for the full GST model, shows that, in the full model, goal strain and unjust strain had only minimal effects on delinquency and aggression. In contrast, negative life-events and victimization were criminogenic to youths in both countries. That is, these two strains continually have statistically significant and large effects on delinquency and aggression. Although the results seemed to duplicate what we found with the basic GST model, the magnitude of relationships between strain, negative emotions, and delinquency was changed; in some cases, a significant relationship disappeared. According to the classic work of Baron and Kenny (1986), mediating effects are at work.

Table 21 provides a summary of the mediating effects. Looking across this table, one finds that anger and depression significantly mediate all of the strain-delinquency relationships, with one exception: depression did not significantly mediate the strain-aggression relationship. Although most of these mediating effects were only partial and moderate to small, in some instances full mediation was found[47]. For example, unjust strain had a significant effect on hitting someone, but this relationship was reduced to almost zero in the full model. Anger and depression totally mediated the unjust strain-delinquency relationship. Moreover, consistent with GST's proposition that outer-directed emotion (e.g., anger) is related to outer-directed behavior (e.g., hitting someone), the total mediating effect comes mostly through anger. Besides the full mediating effect found in the U.S. sample, some fully mediating effects were found in the Taiwanese sample as well. For example, the goal strain-damaging property relationship was reduced to non-significant levels when anger and depression are included in the model. Table 21 shows that the full mediating effect was mostly through depression for goal strain but through anger for unjust strain.

Although the analysis of mediation seemed to support GST's proposition that negative emotions mediate the strain-delinquency relationship, most of the mediating effects were small; only in the fully mediated situation were strong mediating effects found. Consequently, the result suggested that strain had detrimental impacts on youths

---

[47] In some cases, the direct effects (e.g., goal strain → hitting someone) become negative or larger when anger and depression are incorporated in the model. This phenomenon is called suppression or inconsistent mediation (Davis, 1985). Little and colleagues (2007) grouped suppression under the rubric of "partial mediated relationship;" hence, this study also designates the suppression effect as partial mediation. For more information on suppression, consult Mackinnon, Krull, and Lockwood (2000).

mostly because of strain itself. In addition, the relatively small path coefficients that were found in this study seem to suggest that goal strain and unjust strain may have only limited utility in understanding juvenile delinquency.

Finally, with regard to the last two research questions, which addressed the similarities and differences between the U.S. and Taiwan, Table 22 provides a summary of results obtained with the multiple group analysis. As can be seen, most of the tested paths were similar in the two countries and significant in both. Hence, this study found that the strain-delinquency/aggression relationships were similar in magnitude in the U.S. and Taiwan. However, some differences were also evident. Victimization was significantly related to aggression in both countries, but the magnitude of the relationship differed between the two. The sharpest differences were found in the victimization-alcohol use and the negative life-event-alcohol use relationship. The former was significant only in the U.S. sample but the latter was significant only in the Taiwanese sample. With regard to the strain-negative emotion relationship, strain-anger relationships were different between the U.S. and Taiwan, with negative life-event → anger as the sole exception. The result was that most students in the U.S. are more likely than Taiwanese students to react to the four strains with anger. In contrast, strain-depression relationships were similar in the two samples, with exception of unjust strain → depression. Strains were significantly related to depressive feelings for students in both countries, but the depressive feelings associated with unjust strain were stronger in the U.S. students than in the Taiwanese students.

Table 20 Summary for the Full GST model in the U.S. and Taiwan

Variable	Anger		Depression		Damage property		Hit someone		Alcohol use		Aggression	
	U.S.	Taiwan	U.S.	Taiwan	U.S.	Taiwan	U.S.	Taiwan	U.S.	Taiwan	U.S.	Taiwan
Goal strain	+**	+**	+**	+**	-NS	+NS	-NS	-NS	-NS	-NS	+NS	+**
Unjust strain	+**	+**	+**	+**	-NS	+NS	+NS	+NS	+NS	+NS	+NS	-NS
Negative life-event	+*	+*	+**	+*	+*	+***	+***	+***	+*	+***	+*	+*
Victimization	+**	+***	+***	+***	+***	+***	+***	+***	+**	-NS	-NS	-NS
Anger					+**	+**	+**	+***	+***	+***	+***	+***
Depression					+**	+**	+**	+*	+***	+*	+NS	+NS

+ = positive effect. - = negative effect.

NS = non-significant. * = significant at .05 level. ** = significant at .01 level.

Table 21 Summary for the Indirect Effect of Anger and Depression in the U.S. and Taiwan

Path	Damage property		Hit someone		Alcohol use		Aggression	
	U.S.	Taiwan	U.S.	Taiwan	U.S.	Taiwan	U.S.	Taiwan
Goal strain → anger/depression	*(p)(a)	*(t)(d)	*(p)(a)	*(p)(a)	*(p)(s)	*(p)(d)	*(p)(a)	*(p)(a)
Unjust strain → anger/depression	*(p)(a)	*(t)(a)	*(p)(a)	*(p)(a)	*(p)(s)	*(t)(d)	*(p)(a)	*(p)(a)
Negative life-event → anger/depression	*(p)(s)	*(p)(a)	*(p)(s)	*(p)(a)	*(p)(s)	*(p)(d)	*(p)(a)	*(p)(a)
Victimization →anger/depression	*(p)(a)	*(p)(a)	*(p)(a)	*(p)(a)	*(p)(a)	*(p)(a)	*(p)(a)	*(p)(a)

*Indirect effect is significant at .05 level.

p = partial mediation. t = total mediation.

a = most of the mediating effect is from anger. d = most of mediating effect is from depression. s = effects are similar.

The bottom part of Table22 gives the results of testing for similarities for the indirect effects. The summary shows that the indirect effects of goal strain and unjust strain through anger on all four outcome variables were different between the U.S. and Taiwan, and the differences were mostly due to stronger indirect effects in the U.S. In addition, differences were also found in the indirect effects of victimization on aggression and damaging property through anger. Thus, all the differences with regard to indirect effects of victimization were related to anger.

Discussion of the findings

Strain and its characteristics

Agnew (2006a) recently identified some strains that are most likely to be related to delinquency. Victimization, which is on the list, was found in this study to be criminogenic to youths in both the U.S. and Taiwan. In contrast, negative life-events, although not on the list, was also found to be strongly related to youthful delinquency in previous studies (Aseltine & Gore, 2000; Hoffmann & Cerbone, 1999; Hoffmann et al, 2000) as well as in the present study, a result that only partially supports the recent revision of GST; however, the usefulness of GST in explaining juvenile delinquency and its generality are confirmed. Although this strain, as well as victimization, and the relationship of both of these two strains to negative emotions and delinquency, are different in some respects, the negative impacts they have on youths in both countries are unquestioned. These findings are especially important because Cohen (1994) and others (Robinson & Lavin, 1997) argued that external replications, studies that investigate the

179

same research questions but with different subjects, is the only way to provide generalizability and is invaluable for accumulating knowledge in a given domain.

Agnew (2006a) argued that strains are criminogenic if they are seen as "high in magnitude" and "unjust," are "associated with low social control," and create "some pressure or incentive for criminal coping" (Agnew, 2006a, pp. 58-68). After providing these characteristics of strain, Agnew gave a list of strain that possessed these characteristics, hence, criminogenic. Although giving the characteristics of strain (e.g., magnitude) and the list of criminogenic strain enhance GST on the theoretical ground, close scrutiny may raise some challenges. One challenge is that the purpose of providing the four characteristics was to counter the "unfalsifiable" accusation (Jensen, 1995). The listing of criminogenic strains may increase confusion rather than clarification. For example, one would question whether direct measurement of the characteristics of strain is necessary because the listed strains, according to Agnew, already include these characteristics. As in this study, the characteristics of strain were not measured directly, but the criminogenic strain—victimization—was included, which contains all the listed characteristics. To stick with the list of criminogenic strain will once again lead researchers back to the previous state; that is, GST is "unfalsifiable" because one may always find a strain that is related to delinquency but is not on the list. For example, the list did not include negative life-events, but this strain has been found to be related to delinquency in many previous studies as well as in the present study.

180

Table 22 Summary for the Tested Similarities and Differences in the Full GST Model between the U.S. and Taiwan

Path (strain and negative emotions to delinquency and aggression)	Result
Goal strain → damage property	+NS
Unjust strain → damage property	-NS
Negative life-event → damage property	+**
Unjust strain → hit someone	+NS
Negative life-event → hit someone	+**
Victimization → hit someone	-**
Anger → hit someone	+**
Goal strain → alcohol use	+NS
Unjust strain → alcohol use	+NS
Victimization → alcohol use	-**(U.S. only)
Anger → alcohol use	+**
Depression → alcohol use	+**
Goal strain → aggression	+*
Unjust strain → aggression	+NS
Negative life-event → aggression	-*(Taiwan only)
Victimization → aggression	-**
Path (strain to negative emotions)	
Goal strain → anger	-**
Unjust strain → anger	-**
Negative life-event → anger	+**
Victimization → anger	-**
Goal strain → depression	+**
Unjust strain → depression	-**
Negative life-event → depression	+**
Victimization → depression	+**
Path (indirect effect)	
Goal strain→anger→damage property	-*
Unjust strain→anger→damage property	-*
Victimization→anger→damage property	-*
Unjust strain→depression→damage property	-*
Goal strain→anger→hit someone	-*
Unjust strain→anger→hit someone	-*
Goal strain→anger→alcohol use	-*
Unjust strain→anger→alcohol use	-*
Victimization→anger→alcohol use	-*
Goal strain→anger→aggression	-*
Unjust strain→anger→aggression	-*
Victimization→anger→aggression	-*

+ = path is similar. - = path is different

* = the path is significant at .05 level. ** = the path is significant at .01 level.

Another issue related to the above argument is that unjust strain, as measured in the present study, has relatively little effect on delinquency and aggression. This raises yet another challenge to GST because one of the characteristics of criminogenic strain is unjust. Comparing the measurements used in this study and in that of Moon et al. (2008) with Agnew's (2006a) argument on unjust strain, many similarities were found. For example, Agnew suggested that a strain is more likely to be seen as unjust when "victims believe the strain they experienced is *undeserved*" or "the strain strongly *violates strongly held social norms or values*" (pp. 63-64, emphasis in origin). Moon and colleagues (2008) took the former approach by asking students to rate whether they deserve the strain or not; and the present study took the latter approach by presenting statements that violates norms or rules (e.g., imbalance of input/gain). Both studies failed to find that unjust strain was criminogenic, as GST would predict. With regard to the findings of Moon et al., the explanation might be that victimization itself is so negative to students that it leads to delinquency whether it is unjust or not. Hence, measuring the characteristics of such a strain may be redundant[48]. With regard to the present finding, the explanation is that many of the unjust strain statements are related to situations that are least likely to cause crime (e.g., unpopular with peers, demands associated with conventional pursuit) (Agnew, 2006a, pp. 75-77). Incidents related to conventional pursuits that are in themselves unlikely to cause crime may be less criminogenic to youths even if they are seen as unjust. Together, these results may suggest that researchers should probably focus on directly

---

[48] The redundant criticism is also found in Slocum et al. (2005) but with a somewhat different purpose; theirs was to evaluate various dimensions of one of the four characteristics, magnitude.

measuring the characteristics of strain that Agnew gave, but at the same time we should use the listed crimnogenic strains as a guide to guard against redundancy.

Notwithstanding Agnew's revision and above arguments, another possible extension of GST is to consider the hierarchical order of strain. Maslow (1970) argued long ago that human needs constitute a hierarchy; that is, one first satisfies the lower ranking needs and then moves up. The basic needs, physical needs, must be fulfilled before one shows concern about his or her safety needs and other higher ranking needs/success (e.g., love and belonging, esteem). Victimization is criminogenic because such an incident threatens one of the lower ranking needs, safety. One of the focal strains in classic strain theory, strain related to monetary needs, which earlier research had found to be criminogenic (Agnew, 1994; Agnew, Mathews, Bucher, Welcher & Keyes, 2008; Baron, 2004), can be seen as a threat to the very bottom of the hierarchy of human needs, physical needs (e.g., food). This may better account for many cross cultural similarities because strains that threaten the lowest ranked needs would be universally stressful, which in turn would lead to antisocial behavior because individuals want to satisfy such need in an expedient way, which is usually criminal. Therefore, one of the characteristics of strain might be its rank on the hierarchy of needs; the lower the rank the more criminogenic it might be.

Negative emotions

The measure of anger in the present study is situational. Recent arguments from the GST literature have suggested that a situational or state-like measure of negative

183

emotion is better than a trait-like measure (Agnew, 2006b; Capowich et al., 2001; Mazerolle et al., 2003). Mazerolle et al. (2003, p.131) stated that "the relationship between anger and deviant outcomes is attenuated when trait-based measures of anger are used." The same may be true of other negative emotions as well. On this score, Agnew (2006a, 2006b) suggested that the proper test of GST requires researchers to incorporate emotional states. Consistent with these suggestions, anger, measured in the present study, not only affected delinquency and aggression but also mediated the strain-delinquency/aggression relationship. On the other hand, depression, in the present study, as measured by the depressive symptom check-list, which is considered a trait-like measure, also exerts strong effects on delinquency as well as mediating the strain-delinquency relationship. However, in most cases, anger had a stronger mediating effect than depression had. This may support the argument that a state-like measure of negative emotions is more important and appropriate than a trait-like measure.

Although the results of this study seem to advocate acceptance of Agnew's and others' arguments on the situational measure of negative emotions, several challenges arise. First, while the above results seem to support the distinction between state-like and trait-like measures, the differences between the effects of anger and depression on delinquency and between their mediating effects are not large. Most of the state vs. trait argument derives from one negative emotion, anger. Whether such an argument can be extended to other negative emotions is an open question. At present, this may not apply to depression, because this study did not find a large difference between the direct and indirect effects that anger and depression have on delinquency. For example, depression and anger both have statistically significant effects on all delinquent acts, except aggression, which is only related to anger. In addition, the results show that anger and depression exert similar mediating effects on strain-delinquency relationships. Previous studies using similar measures of depression also found that depression is related to delinquency (Beyers & Loeber, 2003; Lin, in press) and that it mitigates the strain-delinquency relationship (Carson et al., 2009; Hoffmann & Su, 1998; Lin et al., 2011; Walls et al., 2007). Hence, some negative emotions can perhaps be distinguished on the basis of being situational or dispositional; other negative emotions may not be so clearly differentiated on this issue, especially those negative emotions related to clinical diagnosis.

Second and related challenge arose from a study that was conducted by Ganem (2008), who used several different scenarios to capture several negative emotional states and used these measures to examine the role of negative emotions in GST. One of her conclusions was that human emotions often occurred together; that is, even with a properly delineated scenario, subjects reported different negative emotions other than the sole emotion that the scenario was supposed to induce. The problem of co-occurrence was found in previous studies (Sharp et al., 2005; Sharp et al., 2001; Sigfusdottir et al., 2004) and in the present study, within which anger and depression were correlated. Hence, there might be a more complex relationship between strain, negative emotion, and delinquency than GST has offered (see Sharp et al., 2001).

Besides the co-occurrence of negative emotions, which may hinder the proper measurement of negative emotions, research from other areas (e.g., psychology) has

185

found that mood is not static but dynamic during adolescent years. For example, Schneiders and colleagues (2007) used the Experience Sampling Method to "collect data from participants at selected moments during their daily activities" (pp.703-704). They found that mood changed across location and social context. As such, the above measurement issue of negative emotion might not be simply a state vs. trait dichotomy.

A third, and more fundamental challenge, is explaining that the role of negative emotions in GST. Many of the strain-delinquency relationships could be explained from many different viewpoints (Agnew, 2001). For example, the victimization-delinquency relationship can be explained by low self-control theory (Schreck, 1999; Schreck, Stewart, & Fisher, 2006). Schreck (1999) has argued that individuals with low self-control are more likely to commit crimes but also more likely to become victims because they are highly likely to be in situations where they will be victimized. One way to distinguish between equally valid theoretical explanations is the inclusion of negative emotion. This inclusion clearly delineates the mechanism linking independent variable (strain) to the outcome (delinquency). In contrast to most mainstream criminological theories (e.g., self-control, social learning), GST is the only theory that takes into account negative emotions and the linkage of strain, negative emotions and delinquency. Hence, for example, victimization leads to negative emotion, which in turn leads to delinquency; this separates GST from other theories.

Although negative emotion provides clear mechanism linking strain to delinquency, vagueness surrounds the role of negative emotion. From the earlier version of GST (Agnew, 1992) to the recent revision (Agnew, 2001, 2006a), GST has never

186

clearly stated whether one should expect a full mediation or only a partial mediation from negative emotions, although the recent revision seems to suggest a full mediation effect (Agnew, 2006a, p.19, Figure 1.1). If this is the theoretical argument of GST, the present study would reject GST's proposition, as would other studies (Aseltine, et al., 2000; Brezina, 2001; Hay, 2003; Hay & Evans, 2006; Mazerolle & Maahs, 2000; Perez, Jennings, & Gover, 2008). However, on some occasions, Agnew has argued that the same coping strategies are used to deal with both strain and negative emotions. Hence, strain remains a potent risk factor for delinquency. The accumulated evidence (Broidy, 2001; Gibson et al., 2001; Jang & Johnson, 2003) and the results from this study seem to support this theoretical argument.

The final challenge is the domain matching or specificity argument. Agnew (2006a, 2006b) argued that researchers should explore how a specific strain may be related to specific negative emotions, which in turn lead to specific forms of delinquency. The first part of this argument refers to the strain-negative emotion relationship and the second part refers to the negative emotion-delinquency relationship. Agnew (1992, p.60) provided a clear delineation of the second part. Outer-directed negative emotions (e.g., anger) were most likely to be related to outer-directed delinquency (e.g., aggression), and inner-directed negative emotions (e.g., depression) were more likely to be related to inner-directed deviance (e.g., substance use). The present study provided only limited support for this assertion. On the one hand, anger was found to be related to both outer- (e.g., hitting someone) and inner-directed delinquency (e.g., alcohol use), and depression was found to be a predictor of both types of delinquency. On the other hand, only anger

187

was related to aggression. However, as explained in the previous chapter, this mismatch has been found by other researchers (Beyers & Loeber, 2003; Terrell et al., 2006). In contrast, Jang and Johnson (2003) and Ganem (2008) directly tested this domain match hypothesis and found support for it. For example, Jang and Johnson (2003) found that strained individuals were more likely to feel anger, which had stronger effects on fighting than on drug use, whereas depressive mood had the opposite effects on fighting and drug use.

The results from this study and studies of others suggest that the domain match argument might need to be further investigated or revised, so that researchers can anticipate which negative emotions should be related to which type of delinquency. Ganem's conclusion provided a direction for this endeavor. She stated that "certain crimes are positively predicted by certain negative emotions, some are negatively influenced, and some are not influenced at all…" (p.74). In addition, Agnew (2006a) proffered another way to deal with these mixed results. He argued that the objects in a strain situation might engender different forms of delinquency. For example, if people are the cause of one's anger, this anger may increase aggression; in contrast, if objects cause one's anger, damaging property or stealing may be the "ideal" way to cope with anger.

With regard to the first part of the specificity argument, studies from psychology have found that the scripts most likely to induce anger include someone or something interfering with one's plan, someone making a demand offensive to the recipient, an individual feeling that others are trying to harm him or her in some way, or the perception of the disadvantage of unfairness (e.g., procedural justice) (Lazarus, 1999; Shaver,

Schwartz, Krison, & O'Connor, 1987; Bies & Tripp, 2001). The strain measured in the present study contains some of these characteristics; hence, the significant relationship found between strain and anger was expected. On the other hand, the scripts of "sadness" or "depressive mood" include the experience of an undesirable outcome, with the perception that one is either unable to change or one is hopeless to correct the situation, or the experience is perceived as creating irrevocable harm (Lazarus, 1999; Shaver et al., 1987). Negative life-events and victimization fit this description and are related to depression, whereas the other two strains may not include these characteristics. Consequently, the present study seems to reject the specificity argument; in contrast to this conclusion, Ganem's (2008) finding that "certain emotions are more likely than others to occur under certain types of strain" (p.73) seems to support this argument.

The above argument indicates lack of consistency with regard to the results of studies of domain matching assertion. Clearly, future research is needed to clarify the incongruent findings from the present study and previous studies as well as GST's assertion. This may enhance the theoretical development of GST and its usefulness in explaining crime and delinquency.

Similarities and differences in GST across cultures

The multiple group analysis revealed some differences between the samples from two countries. One interesting finding is that the strain-anger relationship differs in most cases between the two countries, in that the magnitude is always higher in the U.S. sample than in the Taiwanese sample. This difference is consistent with Heine (2008,

189

p.352), who concluded that "[l]ooking at emotional experience, there is more evidence for cultural diversity." Markus and Kitayama (1994) stated that in an individualistic culture, negative emotion that is related to self (e.g., goal, self identity) is more likely to be felt and expressed. Goal strain, unjust strain, and victimization threaten an individual in various ways (e.g., blocking goals, harming oneself), which increases anger. In addition, Chinese students often attribute their failures to themselves but their successes to the group (Heine, 2008; Heine et al., 2001; Yang, 1986; Yu, 1996); this self-attribution might make one attribute the strain experience to oneself, which in turn could lead to lower anger, because anger is more likely when one has external attributions. One study has documented that many Chinese immigrants have maintained the traditional Chinese culture and parenting practices (Wu, 1996), so the cultural differences in the strain-anger relationship may suggest that applying GST to these and other collectivistic cultures needs to be done with caution.

Another explanation of the difference may be that the Chinese are socialized at an early age to control affective display (Wu, 1996). As reviewed earlier, in a collectivistic culture, great effort is made to maintain social harmony; hence, expressing negative emotions, especially anger, may be prohibited because of its potential to damage interpersonal relationships. Consequently, Taiwanese students might be just as likely to *experience* anger as their counterparts in the U.S. but may prefer not to disclose it. The reluctance to express negative emotions is even more so when these emotions incur great social stigma, such as depression (Russell & Yik, 1996). Moreover, the unwillingness in the Chinese culture to express negative emotions is also evident in the mediating effects

190

that anger and depression have on strain-delinquency relationships; in most cases, if not all, the mediating effects are larger in the U.S. than in the Taiwanese sample.

Another interesting difference that emerged in the multiple group analysis is that the victimization-alcohol use relationship is significant only in the U.S. As explained previously, this might be due to the drinking norms that regulate alcohol use in Taiwan, combined with a living environment that makes excessive use difficult. The difference found for this particular case indicates that it may be useful to include macro social factors (e.g., cultural norms) in the GST (Agnew, 2006a).

The negative life-events-aggression relationship was significant only in the Taiwanese sample; this is interesting, because one would expect Chinese students to have lower aggression levels than students in the U.S. An early study (Ho, 1984) showed that Chinese parents instill impulse control in their children and are less tolerant of aggressive behavior than U.S. parents. One possibility is that the control that Chinese parents exercise over their children is intended to limit their aggression against out-group individuals, but not in-group individuals, because of the fear of retaliation. The aggression measured in the present study was restricted to physical aggression against one's siblings, and aggression against one's own siblings might not be thought of as serious. Moreover, a phenomenon in Chinese culture is that parents emphasize school achievement during their children's adolescent years and tend to be lenient about other behavior, which may lead to greater physical aggression against siblings in the Taiwan.

Aside from the differences noted in this study, some similarities were also found. Students who have experienced more negative life-events and victimization incidents are more likely to hit someone and damage property, regardless of which country they live in. These findings support the generality of GTS and confirm that both negative life-events and victimization have negative impacts on youths. The recent surge of school violence and bullying in Taiwan might be explained by studies based on GST.

Anger, despite the already discussed great cultural differences, has similar effects across countries on alcohol use and on hitting someone. This may be contradictory to the discussion of effects of cultural differences on negative emotion expression. One explanation is that the Chinese, although indeed reluctant to express anger or depression in general, do, however, express these emotions in the same ways as their counterparts in other countries.

Similarities may become the case in situations in which the cultural differences are gradually fading. Scholars have documented that as a country moves greater development, individuals become more individualistic (Trandi, 1995; Hofsted, 2001). In Taiwan, for example, as it advanced to becoming a developed country and was greatly influenced by western culture, the traditional ethos has gradually faded (Smith & Hung, 2005). Lin and Mieczkowski (2011) argued that globalization and free trade have accented the impact of Western culture on the traditional culture; thus, the collectivistic and Confucian mentality has diminished notably. This, in turn, leads Taiwanese adolescents to be more westernized and thus be vulnerable to a similar strain-delinquency mechanism. However, the influence of traditional culture on students has not lost its grip

192

altogether. As such, students in Taiwan have become more westernized but still retain traditional thought.

Some studies have found that individuals in Taiwan hold both individualistic and collectivistic self or bi-cultural self images (Lu & Yang, 2006; Lu, 2008; Lu, Kao, Chang, Wu, & Jin, 2008). Consequently, students in modern Taiwan not only consider similar strains as stressful but also replicate the behavior of their counterparts in the U. S. with regard to the ways in which they cope with strains and negative emotions. The bi-cultural explanation is only tentative, future studies may want to measure both individualistic and collectivistic self of Taiwanese students, and comparing the GST process between students who are high on individualistic self (westernized) but low on collectivistic self, students who are high on collectivistic self (traditional) but low on collectivistic self, and students who are high on both. This may empirically evaluate the bi-culture self and westernization arguments.

Another possible factor that contributes to the development of the bi-cultural self is the low birth rate in Taiwan and the one-child policy in Mainland China. With low birth rate, many couples may have only one child, which may make them spoil their one and only child (Wu, 1996). As a result, the child may develop a high level of individualism early, and thus his or her reactions to strain and negative emotion may become similar to those of children in the U.S. Moreover, as students progress in their schooling, they become more and more individualistic (Greenfield, 1997). Hence, the bicultural phenomenon favors the application of western-developed theories in Taiwan and other eastern developed countries. Finding similarities and cross-cultural supportive results for the theories may become more common in the future.

Limitations of the present study and future study

Although this study is valuable and contributes to the literature on GST, several limitations need to be addressed. First, the characteristics of strain (e.g., magnitude, related to low social control) were not measured directly, and although some researchers suggested that inclusion of the characteristics has limited utility (Botchkovar et al., 2009; Lin & Mieczkowski, 2011), others have found that these characteristics provided the prediction of delinquency (Moon et al., 2008; Slocum et al., 2005).

Second, the depression measure in this study is not ideal. Depression is measured through four questions commonly used in depression symptom check-lists. Whether this should be seen as a situational or dispositional measure is not clear. For example, physicians often use symptoms to diagnose one's health condition, which may render the symptoms as indictors of one's current state of health. On the other hand, these symptoms usually last for some time, so that they can be qualified as an indicator of some illness. Hence, symptoms might include characteristics of both state-like and trait-like measures of negative emotions. A recent study argued that, because depression should be treated as a clinical disorder from the health perspective, distinguishing between state- and trait-depression is problematic (Manasse & Ganem, 2009). Hence, although the measure is not ideal, it was still found to have strong effects on delinquency and in mediating the strain-delinquency relationships.

194

Third, this study measures only anger and depression; other negative emotions, such as fear, anxiety or shame, need to be included. This is especially important given that different cultures may have different focal negative emotions. For example, shame may be the most commonly felt negative emotion for Taiwanese students (Fung & Chen, 2001), but anger may be the regular emotional reaction to strain in the U.S.

Fourth, another important component in the GST consists of the conditioning factors. Agnew (2006a) has argued that whether individuals cope with strain in a delinquent manner depends on these conditioning factors, but the literature contains mixed results in this regard (Baron, 2004, 2007; Baron & Hartnagel, 2002; Mazerolle, Burton, Cullen, Evans, & Payne, 2000; Eitle & Turner, 2002, 2003). In addition, it is statistically difficult to find conditioning effects with the use of survey data (McClelland & Judd, 1993) and to implement them in the SEM approach[49].

Finally, the data are only cross-sectional; hence, this study cannot firmly establish the causal relationship between variables. However, the path analysis used in this study is meant to evaluate causal patterns; thus, the results can at least indicate where to look for causal relationships among variables. Consistent with the causal relationship found in this study, Agnew and White (1992), who used longitudinal data, also found similar results. Moreover, the measurement of variables other than delinquency has no time limit, whereas questions about delinquent behaviors asked subjects about their involvement in these delinquent acts during the past one year only. This provides some control for the

---

[49] In Mplus, a random coefficient has been used to model the conditioning effect when the interaction is between latent variable. However, there is not much research on this issue so far.

temporal order problem. Some scholars have argued that the relationships between strain, negative affect, and reactions are fairly simultaneous (Agnew 1992; Piquero & Sealock 2000, 2004). Notwithstanding the limitation, longitudinal data are still needed to replicate the present path model in order to confirm the findings found in this study.

One related limitation is that the U.S. sample was collected more than a decade ago. Hence, it might be unwise to compare those data to the recent data from Taiwan. However, this may be a desired feature rather than a limitation. The U.S. was more developed than Taiwan was a decade ago[50] but the difference today is smaller. Consequently, comparing these two datasets should not cause too great a problem.

Future research can build upon the present study in several ways. First, characteristics of strain may need to be measured directly. This may help to clarify the challenges raised by results of this study and other studies. Second, a recent study argued that depression measured by means of a clinical symptom checklist should be regarded as trait-depression, and that consequently, the relationship between strain and trait-like depression is moderating rather than mediating (Manasse & Ganem, 2009). Future studies may need to examine this argument when the measure of negative emotion is trait-like. Such studies could greatly advance GST by clarifying the role of negative emotions in GST. Also, future studies should consider the co-occurrence of negative emotions and to model this complex strain-negative emotion-delinquency relationship

---

[50] The comparison was based on annual personal income. In the U.S., the annual personal income was about $28,000 in 1999 (U.S. Census Bureau, 2011), when the Largo survey was conducted, and was $39,000 in 2009. The same number was $16,000 in Taiwan in 2010 (Directorate-General of Budget, Accounting, and Statistics, Executive Yuan, R.O.C., 2011).

directly. Finally, direct comparison across cultures provides a valuable way to extend criminological theories in general and GST in particular. Without such efforts, any generality as well as possible differences in the theoretical mechanisms may not be discovered.

In conclusion, although previous studies may have come to the same conclusion that the present study provides, the lack of direct comparison prevents these studies from giving firm conclusion. This research contributes to the current GST literature by directly comparing and contrasting the GST model in the U.S. and Taiwan. The results show that GST is useful in explaining juvenile delinquency in both the U.S., a more individualistic culture, and Taiwan, a more collectivistic culture. In addition, this study found that victimization and negative life-events are criminogenic to youths; hence, future studies that do not include these two strains may risk of model misspecification. Anger and depression are found to be detrimental to youths in both countries not only because they affect adolescents' wellbeing but also because they lead to delinquent coping strategies. Consequently, these two negative emotions should be incorporated into the GST model.

REFERENCES

Abraham, T., & Russell, D. W. (2004). Missing data: A review of current methods and applications in epidemiological research. *Current Opinion in Psychiatry, 17,* 315-321.

Adèr, H. J., Mellenbergh, G. J., & Hand, D. J. (2008). *Advising on research method: A consultant's companion.* Huizen, Ntherlands: Johannes van Kessel.

Adler, F. (1996). Our American Society of Criminology, the world, and the state of the art- The American Society of Criminology 1995 presidential address. *Criminology, 34,* 1-9.

Agnew, R. (1984). Goal achievement and delinquency. *Sociology and social research, 68,* 435-451.

_____ (1985a). A revised strain theory of delinquency. *Social Forces,* 64, 151-167.

_____ (1985b). Neutralizing the impact of crime. *Criminal Justice and Behavior, 12,* 221-239.

_____ (1987). On "testing structural strain theories." *Journal of Research in Crime and Delinquency, 24,* 281-286.

_____ (1989). A longitudinal test of the revised strain theory. *Journal of Quantitative Criminology, 5,* 373-387.

_____ (1991). Strain and subcultural crime theory. In J. Sheley (Ed.), *Criminology: A contemporary handbook.* Belmont, CA: Wadsworth.

_____ (1992). Foundation for a general strain theory of crime and delinquency. *Criminology, 30,* 47-87.

_____ (1993). Why do they do it? An examination of the intervening mechanisms between social control variables and delinquency. *Journal of Research in Crime and Delinquency, 30,* 245-266.

_____ (1994). Delinquency and the desire for money. *Justice Quarterly, 11,* 411-427.

198

_____ (1997). Stability and change in crime over the life course: A strain theory explanation. In T. P. Thornberry (Vol. Ed.), *Developmental theories of crime and delinquency: Vol. 7. Advances in criminological theory* (pp.101-132). New Brunswick, NJ: Transaction.

_____ (2001). Building on the foundation of general strain theory: Specifying the types of strain most likely to lead to crime and delinquency. *Journal of Research in Crime and Delinquency, 38,* 319-361.

_____ (2002). Experienced, vicarious, and anticipated strain: An exploratory study on physical victimization and delinquency. *Justice Quarterly, 19, 603-632.*

_____ (2003). An integrated theory of adolescent peak in offending. *Youth & Society, 34,* 263-299.

_____ (2005). *Juvenile delinquency: Causes and control* (2nd ed.). Los Angeles, CA: Roxbury.

_____ (2006a). *Pressured into crime: An overview of general strain theory.* LA: Roxbury Publishing Co.

_____ (2006b). General strain theory: Current status and direction. In F. T. Cullen, J. P. Wright, & K. R. Blevins (Eds.), *Taking stock: The status of criminological theory: Vol. 15. Advances in criminological theory* (pp.101-123). New Brunswick: Transaction.

Agnew, R., & Brezina, T. (1997). Relational problems with peers, gender, and delinquency. *Youth & Society, 29,* 84-111.

Agnew, R., Cullen, F. T., Burton, V. S., Jr., Evans, T. D., & Dunaway, R. G. (1996). A new test of classic strain theory. *Justice Quarterly, 13,* 681-704.

Agnew, R., Matthews, S. K., Bucher, J., Welcher, A. N., & Keyes, C. (2008). Socioeconomic status, economic problems, and delinquency. *Youth & Society, 40,* 159-181.

Agnew, R., & White, H. R. (1992). An empirical test of general strain theory. *Criminology, 30,* 475-499.

Akers, R. L. (2000). *Criminological theories: Introduction, evaluation, and application* (3rd ed.). Los Angeles, CA: Roxbury.

Akers, R. L., & Cochran, J. K. (1985). Adolescent marijuana use: A test of three theories of deviant behavior. *Deviant Behavior, 6,* 323-346.

Anderson, E. (1999). *Code of the street.* New York, NY: W.W. Norton & Company.

Aseltine, R. H., Jr., & Gore, S. L. (2000). The variable effects of stress on alcohol use from adolescence to early adult. *Substance & Misuse, 35,* 643-668.

Aseltine, R. H., Jr., Gore, S. L., & Gordon, J. (2000). Life stress, anger, anxiety, and delinquency: An empirical test of general strain theory. *Journal of Health and Social Behavior, 41,* 256-275.

Allison, P. D. (2002). *Missing data.* Sage University Paper Series on Quantitative Applications in the Social Sciences, 07-136. Thousand Oaks, CA: Sage.

_____ (2003). Missing data techniques for structural equation modeling. *Journal of Abnormal Psychology, 112,* 545-557.

Bao, Wang-Ning, Haas, A., & Pi, Y. (2007). Life strain, coping, and delinquency in the People's Republic of China: An empirical test of general strain theory from a matching perspective in social support. *International Journal of Offender Therapy and Comparative Criminology, 51,* 9-24.

Baron, R. M., & Kenny, D. A. (1986). The moderator-mediator variable distinction in social psychological research: Conceptual, strategic, and statistical considerations. *Journal of Personality and Social Psychology, 51,* 1173-1182.

Baron, S. W. (2004). General strain, street youth and crime: A test of Agnew's revised theory. *Criminology, 42,* 457-483.

_____ (2006). Street youth, strain theory, and crime. *Journal of Criminal Justice, 34,* 209-223.

_____ (2007). Stress youth, gender, financial strain, and crime: Exploring Broidy and Agnew's extension to general strain theory. *Deviant Behavior, 28,* 273-302.

_____ (2009). Street youths' violent responses to violent personal, vicarious, and anticipated strain. *Journal of Criminal Justice, 37,* 442-451.

Baron, S. W., & Hartnagel, T. F. (1997). Attributions, affect, and crime: Street youths' reactions to unemployment. *Criminology, 30,* 519-533.

_____ (2002). Street youth and labor market strain. *Journal of Criminal Justice, 30,* 519-533.

Beck, A. T., Steer, R. A., & Brown, G. K. (1996). *Manual for the Beck depression inventory- II.* San Antonio, TX: Psychological Corporation.

Bellah, R. N., Madsen, R., Sullivan, W. M., Swidler, A., & Tipton, S. M. (1996). *Habits of the heart: Individualism and commitment in American life.* Los Angeles, CA: University of California Press.

Bernard, T. J. (1984). Control criticisms of strain theories: An assessment of theoretical and empirical adequacy. *Journal of Research in Crime and Delinquency, 21,* 353-372.

_____ (1987). Replay to Agnew. *Journal of Research in Crime and Delinquency, 24,* 287-290.

Beyers, J. M., & Loeber, R. (2003). Untangling developmental relations between depressed mood and delinquency in male adolescents. *Journal of Abnormal Child Psychology, 31,* 247-266.

Bies, R. J., & Tripp, T. M. (2001). A passion for justice: The rationality and morality of revenge. In R. Cropanzano (Ed.), *Justice in the workplace: From theory to practice* (pp.197-208). Mahwah, NJ: Lawrence Erlbaum.

Bond, M. H., & Hwang, K. K. (1986). The social psychology of Chinese people. In M. H. Bond (Ed), *The Psychology of the Chinese People* (pp.107-170). New York, NY: Oxford University Press.

Bond, M. H., Wan, K. C., Leung, K., & Giacalone, R. A. (1985). How are responses to verbal insult related to cultural collectivism and power distance? *Journal of Cross-Cultural Psychology, 16,* 111-127.

Bollen, K. A., & Stine, R. (1990). Direct and indirect effects: classical and bootstrap estimates of variability. *Sociological Methodology, 20,* 115-140.

Botchkovar, E. V., Tittle, C. R., & Antonaccio, O. (2009). General strain theory: Additional evidence using cross-cultural data. *Criminology, 47,* 131-176.

Brandt, D. (2006). *Delinquency, development, and social policy: Current perspective in psychology.* New Haven, CT: Yale University Press.

Brezina, T. F. (1998). Adolescent maltreatment and delinquency: A question of intervening processes. *Journal of Research in Crime and Delinquency, 35,* 71-99.

_____ (1999). Teenage violence toward parents as an adaptation of family strain. *Youth & Society, 30*, 416-444.

Broidly, L. M. (2001). A test of general strain theory. *Criminology, 39*, 9-35.

Broidly, L. M., & Agnew, R. (1997). Gender and crime: A general strain theory perspective. *Journal of Research in Crime and Delinquency, 34*, 275-306.

Brown, T. A. (2006). *Confirmatory Factor Analysis: For Applied Research*. New York, NY: The Guilford Press.

Brislin, R. W. (1986). The wording and translation of research instruments. In W. J. Lonner, & J. W. Berry (eds.), *Field methods in cross-cultural research* (pp.137-164). Beverly Hills, CA: Sage.

Burton, V. S., Jr. (1991). Explaining adult criminality: Testing strain, differential association and control theories. Unpublished doctoral dissertation, University of Cincinnati.

Burton, V. S., Jr., & Cullen, F. T. (1992). The empirical status of strain theory. *Journal of crime and Justice, 15*, 1-30.

Campus Security Report Center. (2006). 教育部94學年度各級學校校園事件統計分析報告。 [The statistical report of school incidents of school year 2005]. Available at https://csrc.edu.tw/FileManage.mvc/FrontDetail/184

Cao, L. (2007). Return to normality: Anomie and crime in China. *International Journal of Offender Therapy and Comparative Criminology, 51*, 40-51.

Capowich, G. E., Mazerolle, P., & Piquero, A. (2001). General strain theory, situational anger, and social networks: An assessment of conditioning influences. *Journal of Criminal Justice, 29*, 445-461.

Card, N. A., Stucky, B. D., Sawalani, G. M., & Little, .T. D. (2008). Direct and indirect aggression during childhood and adolescence: A meta-analytic review of gender differences, intercorrelations, and relations to maladjustment. *Child Development, 79*, 1185-1229.

Carson, D., Sullivan C., Cochran, J. K., & Lersh, K. (2009). General strain theory and the relationship between early victimization and drug use. *Deviant Behavior, 30*, 54-88.

Chai, D. H., & Yang, S. L. (1999). Gangs in schools: Problems and resolutions. *Journal of Student Guidance Bimonthly, 65*, 8-17.

Chang, E. C. (2001). A look at the coping strategies and style of Asian Americans: Similar and different? In C. R. Snyder (Ed.), *Coping with stress: Effective people and processes* (pp.222-239). London, UK: Oxford University Press.

Chen, C. W., & Chen, J. Q. (2000). 青少年犯罪成因及預防策略。[Causes of juvenile delinquency and its prevention]. *Criminal Justice Policy & Crime Research, 3,* 113-128.

Chen, J. C. (2000). 青少年生活壓力、家庭氣氛與偏差行為之關係研究。 [A study on the relationship between juvenile life-stress, family atmosphere and delinquency]. Unpublished master thesis, National Changhua University of Education.

Child, D. (2006). *The essential of factor analysis* (3rd ed.). New York, NY: Continuum International.

Chou, C. P., & Bentler, P. M. (1995). Estimates and tests in structural equation modeling. In R. H. Hoyle (Ed.), *Structural equation modeling: Concepts, issues, and applications* (pp.37-55). Thousand Oaks, CA: Sage.

Chun, Chi-Ah, Moons, R. H., & Cronkite, R. C. (2005). Culture: A fundamental context for the stress and coping paradigm. In P. T. P. Wang & L. C. J. Wong (Eds.), *Handbook of multicultural perspectives on stress and coping* (pp.29-53). New York, NY: Springer.

Chu, M. M. (2000). Taiwan. In G. Barak (Ed.), *Crime and crime control: A global view* (pp.199-217). Westport, CT: Greenwood Press.

Chung, T., Langenbucher, J., Labouvie, E., Panadina, R. J., & Moos, R. H. (2001). Changes in alcoholic patients' coping responses predict 12-month treatment outcomes. *Journal of Consulting and Clinical Psychology, 69,* 92-100.

Clinard, M. B. (1964). *Anomie and deviant behavior: A discussion and critique.* New York: The Free Press.

Cloward, R., & Ohlin, L. (1960). Delinquency and opportunity. Golencoe, IL: Free Press.

Cohen, A. K. (1955). *Delinquent boys.* Golencoe, IL: Free Press.

Cohen, J. (1994). The earth is round (p < .05). *American Psychologist, 49,* 997-1003.

_____ (1965). The sociology of the deviant act: Anomie theory and beyond. *American Sociological Review, 30,* 5-14.

Collins, L. M., Schafer, J. L., & Kam, C. M. (2001). A comparison of inclusive and restrictive strategies in modern missing-data procedures. *Psychological Methods, 6,* 330-351.

Colten, M. E., & Gore, S. (1991). *Adolescent Stress: Causes and Consequences.* New York: Aldine De Gruyter.

Compas, B. E., & Wanger, B. M. (1991). Psychosocial stress during adolescence: Intrapersonal and interpersonal processes. In M. E. Colten & S. Gore (Eds.), *Adolescent stress: Causes and Consequences* (pp. 67-92). New York: Aldine De Gruyter.

Copper, J. F. (2003). *Taiwan: Nation-state or province?* Cambridge, MA: Westview.

Crime Investigation Bureau. (2008). 犯罪預防。[Crime prevention]. Available at http://www.cib.gov.tw/crime/Crime_Book.aspx

Cross, S. E. (1990). *The role of the self-concept in cross-cultural adaptation.* Unpublished doctoral dissertation, University of Michigan.

Cullen, F. T. (1984). *Rethinking crime and deviance theory: The emergence of a structuring tradition.* Totowa, NJ: Rowman & Allanheld.

Cullen, F. T., Wright, J. P., & Blevins, K. R. (2006). *Taking Stock: The Status of Criminological Theory.* New Brunswick, NJ: Transaction Publishers.

Dai, Y. (2005). The development of E-Scooter in Taiwan. *E-Scooter Industry Periodical, 7,* 2-4.

Davis, J. A. (1985). The logic of causal order. Sage University Paper Series on Quantitative Applications in the Social Sciences, 07-055. Thousand Oaks, CA: Sage.

De Coster, S., & Kort-Butler, L. (2006). How general is general strain theory? Assessing determinacy and indeterminacy across life domains. *Journal of Research in Crime and Delinquency, 43,* 297-325.

Department of Budget, Accounting and Statistic, Kaohsiung City Government. (2009). 高雄市統計年報。[Kaohsiung city annual statistic report]. Available at http://kcgdg.kcg.gov.tw/book/yearbook/index.htm

Department of Statistics, Ministry of Education. (2008). 教育部教育統計。[Education statistics] Available at http://140.111.34.54./statistics/content.aspx?site_content_sn=8869

_____ (2009). 主要統計表。[Major statistics] Available at http://www.edu.tw/statistics/content.aspx?site_content_sn=8869

Directorate-General of Budget, Accounting, and Statistics, Executive Yuan, R.O.C. (2011). 人口靜態統計。[Statistics of Population]. Available at http://www.dgbas.gov.tw/ct.asp?xItem=15408&CtNode=4594

_____ (2011). 國民所得統計。[Statistics of Personal Income] Available at http://www.stat.gov.tw/ct.asp?xItem=28862&ctNode=3565

Drapela, L. A. (2006). The effect of negative emotion on licit and illicit drug use among high school dropouts: An empirical test of general strain theory. *Journal of Youth and Adolescence, 35,* 755-770.

DuRant, R H., Getts, A., Cadenhead, C., Emans, S. J., & Woods, E. R. (1995). Exposure to violence and victimization and depression, hopelessness, and purpose in life among adolescents living in and around public housing. *Developmental and Behavioral Pediatrics, 16,* 233-237.

Durkheim, E. (1947). *Division of labor in society* (G. Simpson, Trans.) Glencoe, IL: Free Press. (Original work published 1893).

_____ (2006). *On suicide* (R. Buss, Trans.). New York: Penguin Books. (Original work published 1897).

Education Bureau, Kaohsiung City Government. (2010). 教育現況統計。[Current Educational Statistics]. Available at http://163.32.250.1:8000/Members/grp07/new_page_3.htm

Eftekhari, A., Turner, A. P., & Larimer, M. E. (2004). Anger expression, coping, and substance use in adolescent offenders. *Addictive Behaviors, 29,* 1001-1008.

Eitle, D. J. (2002). Exploring a source of deviance-producing strain for females: Perceived discrimination and general strain theory. *Journal of Criminal Justice, 30,* 95-111.

Eitle, D. J., & Turner, R. J. (2002). Exposure to community violence and young adult crime: The effects of witnessing violence, traumatic victimization, and other stressful life events. *Journal of research in Crime and Delinquency, 39,* 214-237.

_____ (2003). Stress exposure, race, and young adult crime. *Sociological Quarterly, 44,* 243-269.

Ekman, P. (1999). Basic emotions. In T. Dalgleish & M. J. Power (Eds.), *Handbook of cogniyion and emotion* (pp.45-60). UK: John Wiley & Sons.

Elliott, D. S. (1994). Serious violent offenders: Onset, developmental course, and termination- The American Society of Criminology 1993 Presidential Address. *Criminology, 32,* 1-21.

Elliott, D. S., Ageton, S. S., & Canter, R. J. (1979). An integrated theoretical perspective on delinquent behavior. *Journal of Research in Crime and Delinquency, 16,* 3-27.

Elliott, D. S., Huizinga, D., & Ageton, S. S. (1985). *Explaining delinquency and drug use.* Thousand Oaks, CA: Sage.

Elliott, D. S., & Voss, H. L. (1974). Delinquent and dropout. Lexington, MA: D. C. Health.

Ellwanger, S. J. (2007). Strain, attribution, and traffic delinquency among young drivers. *Crime & delinquency, 53,* 523-551.

Eve, R. A. (1978). A study of efficacy and interactions of several theories for explaining rebelliousness among high school students. *Journal of Criminal Law and Criminology, 69,* 115-125.

Fabrigar, L. R., Wegener, D. T., MacCallum, R. C., & Strahan, E. J. (1999). Evaluating the use of exploratory factor analysis in psychological research. *Psychological Methods, 4,* 272-299.

Farnworth, M., & Leiber, M. J. (1989). Strain theory revisited: Economic goals, educational means and delinquency. *American Sociological Review, 54,* 263-274.

Farrington, D. P. (1989). Early predictors of adolescent aggression and adult violence. *Violence and Victims, 22,* 79-100.

Florida Department of Law Enforcement. (1999). *Crimes and crime rates statistics* [Data file]. Available at http://fl.rand.org/cgi-bin/annual.cgi

Flora, D. B., & Curran, P. J. (2004). An empirical evaluation of alternative methods of estimation for confirmatory factor analysis with ordinal data. *Psychological Methods, 9,* 466-491.

Ford, J. A., & Schroeder, R. D. (2009). Academic strain and non-medical use of prescription stimulants among college students. *Deviant Behavior, 30,* 26-53.

Fritz, M. S., & MacKinnon, D. P. (2007). Required sample size to detect the mediated effect. *Psychological Science, 18,* 233-239.

Froggio, G. (2007). Strain and juvenile delinquency: A critical review of Agnew's general strain theory. *Journal of Loss and Trauma, 12,* 383-418.

Froggio, G., & Agnew, R. (2007). The relationship between crime and "objective" versus "subjective" strains. *Journal of Criminal Justice, 35,* 81-87.

Fung, H., & Chen, E. C. H. (2001). Across time and beyond skin: Self and transgression in the everyday socialization of shame among Taiwanese preschool children. *Social Development, 10,* 420-437.

Gabrenya, W. K., & Wang, Y. (1983). *Cultural differences in self schemata.* Paper presented at the Southeast Psychological Association Convention, Atlanta, 1983.

Gallois C., Giles, H., Ota, H., Pierson, H. D., Ng, S. H., Lim, T. S., et al. (1996). Intergenerational communication across the Pacific Rim: The impact of filial piety. In H. Grad, A. Blanco, & J. Georgas (Eds.), *Key issues in cross-cultural psychology* (pp.192-211). Lisse, Netherlands: Swets & Zeitlinger.

Gates, H. (1987). *Chinese working-class lives: Getting by in Taiwan.* Ithaca, NY: Cornell University Press.

Ganem, N. M. (2008). *The role of negative emotion in general strain theory: An empirical study.* La Vergne, TN: Lightning Source Inc.

Gibson, C. L., Swatt, M., & Jolicoeur, J. R. (2001). Assessing the generality of general strain theory: The relationship among occupational stress experienced by male police officers and domestic forms of violence. *Journal of Crime and Justice, 24,* 29-57.

Gorsuch, R. L. (1983). *Factor analysis* (2nd ed.). Hillsdale, NJ: Erlbaum.

Gottfredson, M. R., & Hirschi, T. (1990). *A General Theory of Crime.* Stanford, California: Stanford University Press.

Greenfield, P. M. (1997). You can't take with you: Why ability assessments don't cross cultures. *American Psychologist, 52,* 1115-1124.

Harnish, J. D., Aseltine, R. H., Jr., & Gore, S. (2000). Resolution of stressful experience as an indicator of coping effectiveness in young adult: An event history analysis. *Journal of Health and Social Behavior, 41,* 121-136.

Harrell, E. (2007). *Adolescent victimization and delinquency behavior.* New York, NY: LFB.

Harrell, S. (1981). Normal and deviant drinking in rural Taiwan. In A. Kleinman & L. Tsung-Yi (Eds.), *Normal and abnormal behavior in Chinese culture* (pp.49-59). Boston, MA: D. Reidel.

Hatcher, L. (1994). *A step-by-step approach to using SAS system for factor analysis and structural equation modeling.* Cary, NC: SAS Institute.

Hauser, S. T., & Bowlds, M. K. (1990). Stress, coping, and adaption. In S. S. Feldman & G. R. Elliott (Eds), *At the threshold: The developing adolescent* (pp.388-413). Cambridge, MA: Harvard University Press.

Hay, C. (2003). Family strain, gender, and delinquency. *Sociological Perspectives, 46,* 107-135.

Hay, C., & Evans, M. M. (2006). Violent victimization and involvement in delinquency: Examining predictions from general strain theory." *Journal of Criminal Justice, 34,* 261-274.

Hayes, A. F. (2009). Beyond Baron and Kenny: Statistical mediation analysis in the new millennium. *Communication Monographs, 76,* 408-420.

Hegtvedt, K. A. (1990). The effects of relationship structure on emotional response to inequity. *Social Psychology Quarterly, 53,* 214-228.

Heine, S. J. (2008). *Cultural psychology.* New York, NY: W. W. Norton.

Heine, S. J., Kitayama, S., Lehman, D. R., Takata, T., Ide, E., Leung, C., & Matsumoto, H. (2001). Divergent consequences of success and failure in Japan and North America: An investigation of self-improving motivations and malleable selves. *Journal of Personality and Social Psychology, 81,* 599-615.

Heine, S. J., & Lehman, D. R. (1995). Social desirability among Canadian and Japanese students. *Journal of Social Psychology, 135,* 777-779.

Herbert, T. B., & Cohen, S. (1996). Measurement issues in research on psychological stress. In H. B. Kaplan (Ed.), *Psychological stress: perspectives on structure, theory, life-course, and methods* (pp.295-332). New York: Academic Press.

Hirschi, T. (1969). *Causes of delinquency.* Los Angeles, CA: University of California Press.

Ho, H. Z., Chen, W. W., & Kung, H. Y. (2008). Taiwan. In I. Epstein & J. Pattnaik (Eds.), *Asia and Oceania: Vol. 1. The Greenwood encyclopedia of children's issues worldwide* (pp.439-464). Westport, CT: Greenwood Press.

Ho, D. Y. F. (1986). Chinese patterns of socialization: A critical review. In M. H. Bond (Ed), *The Psychology of the Chinese People* (pp.1-37). New York, NY: Oxford University Press.

_____ (1996). Cognitive socialization in Confucian heritage cultures. In P. M. Greenfield & R. R. Cocking (Eds.), *Cross-cultural roots of minority child development* (pp.285-313). Hillsdale, NJ: Lawrence Erlbaum.

_____ (1996). Filial piety and its psychological consequences. In M. H. Bond (Ed.), *The handbook of Chinese psychology* (pp. 155-165). New York, NY: Oxford University Press.

Ho, D. Y. F., & Chiu, C-Y. (1994). Component ideas of individualism, collectivism, and social organization: An application in the study of Chinese culture. In U. Kim, H. C. Triandis, C. Kagitcibasi, S-C. Choi, & G. Yoon (Eds.), *Individualism and collectivism: Theory, method, and applications* (pp.137-156). Thousand Oaks, CA: Sage.

Hoffmann, J. P. (2002). A contextual analysis of differential association, social control and strain theories of delinquency. *Social Forces, 81,* 753-785.

Hoffmann, J. P., & Cerbone, F. G. (1999). Stressful life events and delinquency escalation in early adolescence. *Criminology, 37,* 343-373.

Hoffmann, J. P., Cerbone, F.G., & Su, S. S. (2000). A growth curve analysis of stress and adolescent drug use. *Substance Use & Misuse, 35,* 687-716.

Hoffmann, J. P., & Miller, A. S. (1998). A latent variable analysis of general strain theory. *Journal of Quantitative Criminology, 14,* 83-110.

Hoffmann, J. P., & Su, S. S. (1997). The conditional effects of stress on delinquency and drug use: A strain theory assessment of sex differences. *Journal of Research in Crime and Delinquency, 34,* 46-78.

_____ (1998). Stressful life events and adolescent substance sue and depression: Conditional and gender differentiated effects. *Substance Use & Misuse, 33,* 2219-2262.

Hofstede, G. (2001). *Culture's Consequences* (2nd ed.).Thousand Oaks: Sage Publications.

209

Hofstede, G., & Bond, M. H. (2001). The Confucius Connection: From cultural roots to economic growth. In M. J. Gannon (Ed.), *Cultural metaphors: Readings research translations, and commentary* (pp.31-50). Thousand Oaks, CA: Sage.

Hollist, D. R., Hughes, L. A., & Schaible, L. M. (2009). Adolescent maltreatment, negative emotion, and delinquency: An assessment of general strain theory and family-based strain. *Journal of Criminal Justice, 37,* 379-387.

Hou, C. (2003). 青少年犯罪問題與政策現況。[Current state of juvenile delinquency and policy]. *Criminal Justice Policy & Crime Research, 6,* 131-148.

Hsu, F. L. K. (1983). *Rugged individualism reconsidered: Essay in psychological anthropology.* Knoxville, TN: University of Tennessee Press.

Huang, D. H. (2003). Characteristics and problems for the development of adolescents in Taiwan. In F. Pajares & T. Urdan (Eds.), *International Perspectives on Adolescence* (pp.303-318). Greenwich: Information Age Publishing.

Hui, C. H., & Villareal, M. J. (1989). Individualism –collectivism and psychological needs: Their relationships in two cultures. *Journal of Cross-Cultural Psychology, 20,* 310-323.

Hussong, A. M., & Chassin, L. (1994). The stress-negative affect model of adolescent alcohol use: Disaggregating negative affect. *Journal of Studies on Alcohol, 55,* 707-718.

Hussong, A. M., Hicks, R. E., Levy, S. A., & Curran, P. J. (2001). Specifying the relationship between affect and heavy alcohol use among young adults. *Journal of Abnormal Psychology, 110,* 449-461.

Introduction of Juvenile Guidance Sections. (1991). Taipei, Taiwan (in Mandarin).

James, L. R., & Brett, J. M. (1984). Mediators, moderators, and tests for mediation. *Journal of Applied Psychology, 69,* 307-321.

Jang, S. J. (2007). Gender differences in strain, negative emotions, and coping behaviors: A general strain theory approach. *Justice Quarterly, 24,* 523-553.

Jang, S. J., & Lyons, J. A. (2006). Strain, social support, and retreatism among African Americans. *Journal of Black Studies, 37,* 251-274.

Jang, S. J., & Johnson, B. R. (2003). Strain, negative emotions, and deviant coping among African Americans: A test of general strain theory. *Journal of Quantitative Criminology, 19,* 79-105.

_____ (2005). Gender, religiosity, and reactions to strain among African Americans. *Sociological Quarterly, 46,* 323-357.

Jensen, G. F. (1995). Salvaging structure through strain: A theoretical and empirical critique. In F. Adler & W. S. Laufer (Eds.), *The legacy of anomie theory: Vol. 6. Advances in criminological theory* (pp.139-158). New Brunswick, NJ: Transaction.

Johnson, M. C., & Morris, R. G. (2008). The moderating effects of religiosity on the relationship between stressful life events and delinquent behavior, *Journal of Criminal Justice, 36,* 486-493.

Jones, R. A. (1986). *Emile Durkheim: An introduction to four major works.* Beverly Hill, CA: Sage.

Juvenile Law. (1981). Taipei, Taiwan (in Mandarin).

Kaplan, H. B. (1983). *Psychosocial stress: Trends in theory and research.* New York, NY: Academic Press.

Karmen, A. (2001). Crime victims: An introduction to victimology (4th ed.). Los Angeles, CA: Wadsworth.

Karstedt, S. (2001). Comparing cultures, comparing crime: Challenges, prospects, and problems for a global criminology. *Crime. Law, and Social Change, 36,* 285-308.

Kaufman, J. M. (2009). Gendered responses to serious strain: The argument for a general strain theory of deviance. *Justice Quarterly, 26,* 410-444.

Kohn, M. L. (1987). Cross-national research as an analytic strategy: American Sociological Association, 1987 Presidential Address. *American Sociological Review, 52,* 713-731.

Kim, U., & Choi, S. H. (1994). Individualism, Collectivism, and child development: A Korean perspective. In P. M. Greenfield & R. R. Cocking (Eds.), *Cross-cultural roots of minority child development* (pp.227-257). Hillsdale, NJ: Lawrence Erlbaum.

Kim, U., Triandis, H. C., Kagitcibasi, C., Choi, Sang-Chin, & Yoon, G. (1994). Introduction. In U. Kim, H. C. Triandis, C. Kagitcibasi, Sang-Chin, Choi, & G.

Yoon (Eds.), *Individualism and Collectivism; Theory, Method, and Applications* (pp.1-11). Thousand Oaks: Sage Publications.

Kennedy, L. W., & Baron. S. W. (1993). Routine activities and a subculture of violence: A study of violence on the street. *Journal of Research in Crime and Delinquency, 30,* 88-112.

Kilpatrick, D. G., Saunders, B. E., Veronen, L. J., Best, C. L., & Von, J. M. (1987). Criminal victimization: Lifetime prevalence, reporting to police, and psychological impact. *Crime & Delinquency, 33,* 479-498.

King, A. Y. C. (1981). *Individual and group in Confucianism: A relational perspective.* Paper presented at the Conference on Individualism and Wholism, York, Maine.

King, A. Y. C., & Bond, M. H. (1985). The Confucian paradigm of man: A sociological view. In W. S. Tseng & D. Y. H. Wu (Eds.), *Chinese culture and mental health* (pp.29-45). Orlando, FL: Academic Press.

Kirk, R. E. (1996). Practical significance: A concept whose time has come. *Educational and Psychological Measurement, 56,* 746-759.

Kitsuse, J. I., & Dietrick, D. C. (1959). Delinquent boys: A critique. *American Sociological Review, 24,* 208-215.

Kleinman, A. (1986). *Social origins in distress and disease.* New Haven, NY: Yale University Press.

Kline, R. B. (2005). *Principles and practices of structural equation modeling.* New York, NY: Guilford Press.

Kornhauser, R. R. (1978). *Social sources of delinquency: An appraisal of analytic models.* Chicago, IL: University of Chicago Press.

Kroeber, A. L., & Kluckhohn, C. (1952). *Culture: A critical review of concepts and definitions* (Papers of the Peabody Museum of Archaeology and Ethnology). Cambridge, MA: The Museum.

Kroeber, A. L., & Parsons, T. (1958). The concepts of culture and of social system. *American Sociological Review, 23,* 582-583.

Kuo, J. H., & Wu, H. L. (2003). The placement guidance for delinquent children and youth. *Criminal Justice Policy & Crime Research, 6,* 149-168.

Kuo, S. Y., Cuvelier, S. J., & Chang, K. M. (2009). Explaining criminal victimization in Taiwan: A lifestyle approach. *Journal of Criminal Justice, 37,* 461-467.

Lam, C. M. (2007). *Not growing up forever: A Chinese conception of adolescent development.* New York, NY: Nova Science.

Largo Chamber of Commerce. (1998). *Largo demographics* [Data file]. Available at http://www.largochamber.com

Larson, R., & Asmussen, L. (1991). Anger, worry, and hurt in early adolescence: An enlarging world of negative emotions. In M. E. Colton & S. Gore (Eds.), *Adolescent Stress: Causes and Consequences* (pp. 21-42). New York, NY: Aldine de Gruyter.

Laungani, P. (2004). *Asian perspective in counseling and psychotherapy.* New York, NY: Brunner-Rutledge.

Lauritsen, J. L., Sampson, R. J., & Laub, J. H. (1991). The Link between Offending and Victimization among Adolescents. *Criminology, 29,* 265-292.

Lazarus, R. S. (1991). *Emotion and adaptation.* New York, NY: Oxford University Press.

_____ (1999). *Stress and emotion: A new synthesis.* New York, NY: Springer.

Lee, J. M., Huang, H. L., & Miao, D. F. (2000). 青少年物質使用之社會學習及社會連結因素研究---已在學生為例。[Applying social learning and social bonding on juvenile substance use by using a student sample]. *健康促進暨衛生教育雜誌, 20,* 17-34.

Lee, M., & Larson, R. (2000). The Korean 'examination hell': Long hours of studying, distress, and depression. *Journal of Youth and Adolescence, 29,* 249-271.

Lee, S. X., Lin, G. N., Yang, H. R., Fu, L. A., Liu, X. W., & Lee, S. Q. (2009). A qualitative study of knowledge, attitude, practice, and coping regarding drugs amongst adolescent drug offenders. *Journal of Research in Delinquency and Prevention, 1,* 1-28.

Lee, Y. N. (1998). 校園暴力問題防治方法之探討。[Discussion on the problem of campus violence and its prevention]. *Criminal Justice Policy & Crime Research, 1,* 217-236.

Leung, K., Au, Y. F., Fernandez-Dols, J. M., & Iwawaki, S. (1992). Preference for methods of conflict processing in two collectivist cultures. *International Journal of Psychology, 27,* 195-209.

Leung, K., & Bond, M. H. (1982). How Chinese and Americans reward task-related contributions: A preliminary study. *Psychologia, 25,* 32-39.

Leung, K., & Li, W. K. (1990). Psychological mechanisms of process control effects. *Journal of Applied psychology, 75,* 613-620.

Leung, K. S., Li, J. H., Tsay, W. I., Callahan, C., Liu, S. F., Hsu, J., Hoffer, L., & Cottler, L. B. (2008). Dinosaur girls, candy girls, and trinity: Voices of Taiwanese club drug users. *Journal of Ethnicity in Substance Abuse, 7,* 237-257.

Levin, J. R. (1993). Statistical significance testing from three perspectives. *Journal of Experimental Education, 61,* 378-382.

Li, X. Y., & Chiang, I C. (2001). The study of the subject life stress, social support, coping behaviors and psycho-physical health situation of the junior high school students in Taoyuan. 衛生教育學報, *15,* 115-132.

Lin, C., & Liu, W. T. (1999). Intergenerational relationships among Chinese immigrant families from Taiwan. In H. P. McAdoo (Ed.), *Family ethnicity: Strength in diversity* (pp.271-286). Newbury Park, CA: Sage.

Lin, W. H. (in press). General strain theory in Taiwan: A latent growth curve modeling approach. *Asia Journal of Criminology.*

Lin, W. H., Cochran, J. K., & Mieczkowski, T. (2011). Direct and Vicarious violent victimization and juvenile delinquency: An application of general strain theory. *Sociological Inquiry.*

Lin, W. H., & Mieczkowski, T. (2011). Subjective strains, conditioning factors, and juvenile delinquency: General strain theory in Taiwan. *Asian Journal of Criminology, 6,* 69-87.

Link, T. C. (2008) Adolescent substance use in Germany and the United States: A cross-cultural test if the applicability and generalizability of theoretical indicators. *European Journal of Criminology, 5,* 453-480.

Liska, A. E. (1971). Aspirations, expectations, and delinquency: Stress, and additive models. *Sociological Quarterly, 12,* 99-107.

Little, T. D, Card, N. A., & Bovaird, J. A. (2007). Structural equation modeling of mediation and moderation with contextual factors. In T. D. Little, J. A. Bovaird, & N. A. Card (Eds.), *Modeling Contextual Effects in Longitudinal Studies* (pp. 207-230). Mahwah, NJ: Lawrence Erlbaum.

214

Lonner, W. J. (1994). Culture and human diversity. In E. J. Trickett, R. J. Watts, & D. Brirman (Eds.), *Human diversity: Perspectives on people in context* (pp.230-243). San Francisco, CA: Jossey-Bass.

Lu, L. (2008). The individual-oriented and Social-oriented Chinese bicultural self: Testing the theory. *The Journal of Social Psychology, 148*, 347-373.

Lu, L., Kao, S. F., Chang, T-T, Wu, H-P, & Jin, Z. (2008). The individual- and social-oriented Chinese bicultural self: A subcultural analysis contrasting mainland Chinese and Taiwanese. *Social Behavior and Personality, 36*, 337-346.

Lu, L., & Yang, K. S. (2006). Emergence and composition of the traditional-modern bicultural self of people in contemporary Taiwanese societies. *Asian Journal of Social Psychology, 9,* 167-175.

Ma, A. L. (2000). *The research into the cognition, obeying willingness and behavior of adolescents for Tobacco Hazards Act in Taiwan.* Doctoral dissertation, National Taiwan Normal University.

MacKinnon, D. P., Krull, J. L., & Lockwood, C. M. (2000). Equivalence of mediation, confounding and suppression effect. *Prevention Science, 1*, 173-181.

MacKinnon, D. P., Lockwood, C. M., Hoffman, J. M., West, S. G., & Sheets, V. (2002). A comparison of methods to test mediation and other intervening variable effects. *Psychological Methods, 71*, 83-104.

MacKinnon, D. P., Lockwood, C. M., & Williams, J. (2004). Confidence limits for the indirect effect: Distribution of the product and resampling methods. *Multivariate Behavioral Research, 39,* 99-128.

Manasse, M. E., & Ganem, N. (2009). Victimization as a cause of delinquency: The role of depression and gender. *Journal of Criminal Justice, 37,* 371-378.

Markus, H. R., & Kitayama, S. (1991). Culture and the self: Implications for cognition, emotion, and motivation. *Psychological Review, 20,* 568-579.

_____ (1994). The cultural construction of self and emotion: Implications for social behavior. In S. Kitayama, & H. R. Markus (eds.), *Emotion and cultural: Empirical studies of mutual influence* (pp.89-130). Washington, DC: American Psychology Association.

Maruyama, G. M. (1997). *Basics of Structural equation modeling.* Thousand Oaks, CA: Sage.

Maslow, A. H. (1970). *Motivation and personality*. New York: Harper & Row.

Maxwell, S. (2001). A focus on familial strain: Antisocial behavior and delinquency in Filipino society. *Sociological Inquiry, 71*, 265-292.

Mazerolle, P. (1998). Gender, general strain, and delinquency: An empirical examination. *Justice Quarterly, 15*, 65-91.

Mazerolle, P., Burton, V. S., Cullen, F. T., Evans, D. T., & Payne, G. L. (2000). Strain, anger, and delinquent adoptions: Specifying general strain theory. *Journal of Criminal Justice, 17*, 753-778.

Mazerolle, P., & Maahs, J. (2000). General strain and delinquency: An alternative examination of conditioning influences. *Justice Quarterly, 17*, 753-778.

Mazerolle, P., & Piquero, A. (1997). Violent responses to strain: An examination of conditioning influences. *Violence and Victim, 12*, 323-343.

_____ (1998). Linking exposure to strain with anger: An investigation of deviant adaptations. *Journal of Criminal Justice, 26*, 195-211.

Mazerolle, P., Piquero, A., & Capowich, G. E. (2003). Examining the links between strain, situational and dispositional anger, and crime. *Youth & Society, 35*, 131-157.

McClelland, G. H., & Judd, C. M. (1993). Statistical difficulties of detecting interactions and moderator effects. *Psychological Bulletin, 114*, 376-390.

Mcknight, P. E., Mcknight, K. M., Sidani, S., & Figueredo, A. J. (2007). *Missing data: A gentle introduction*. New York, NY: Guiford.

Merton, R. K. (1938). Social structure and anomie. *American Sociological Review, 54*, 597-611.

_____ (1959). Social structure and anomie: Revisions and extensions. In R. N. Anshen (Ed.), *The family: Its function and destiny: Vol. V. Science of Culture Series* (pp.226-257). New York: Harper & Brothers.

_____ (1964). Anomie, anomia, and social interaction: Contexts of deviant behavior. In M. B. Clinard (Ed.), *Anomie and deviant behavior* (pp.213-242). New York, NY: The Free Press.

_____ (1968). *Social structure and anomie* (Enlarged ed.). New York: The Free Press.

216

Mesquita, B., & Frijda, N. H. (1992). Cultural variations in emotions: A review. *Psychological Bulletin, 112,* 179-204.

Messner, S. F. (1988). Merton's "social structure and anomie": The road not taken. *Deviant Behavior, 9,* 33-53.

Ministry of Justice. (2007). 法務部統計指標 。[Statistical index] Available at http://www. moj.gov.tw/ct.asp?xItem=126021&CtNode=2345&map=001

_____ (2008). 97年少年兒童犯罪概況及其分析。[The current state of juvenile and child delinquency and its analysis]. Available at http://www.criminalresearch.moj.gov.tw/public/Attachment/910719591765.pdf

Mirowsky, J., & Ross, C. E. (1995). Sex difference in distress: Real or artifact? *American Sociological Review, 60,* 449-468.

Moffitt, T. E. (1993). Adolescence-Limited and Life-Course-Persistent antisocial behavior: A developmental taxonomy. *Psychological Review, 100(4), 674-701.*

Moon, B., Blurton, D., & McCluskey, J. D. (2008). General strain theory and delinquency: Focusing on the influences of key strain characteristics on delinquency. *Crime & Delinquency, 54,* 582-613.

Moon, B., Hays, K., & Blurton, D. (2009). General strain theory, key strains, and deviance. *Journal of Criminal Justice, 37,* 98-106.

Moon, B., & Morash, M. (2004). Adaptation of theory for alternative cultural contexts: Agnew's general strain theory in South Korea. *International Journal of Comparative and Applied Criminal Justice, 28,* 77-103.

Moon, B., Morash, M., McCluskey, C. P., & Hwang, H. W. (2009). A comprehensive test of general strain theory: Key strains, situational- and trait-based negative emotions, conditioning factors, and delinquency. *Journal of Research in Crime and Delinquency, 46,* 182-212.

Moore, C. A. (1967). Introduction: The humanistic Chinese mind. In C. A. Moore (Ed.), *The Chinese mind: Essential of Chinese philosophy and culture* (pp.1-10). Honolulu, HI: University of Hawaii Press.

Morash, M., & Moon, B. (2007). Gender differences in the effects of strain on the delinquency of South Korean youth. *Youth & Society, 38,* 300-321.

Mu, R. H. (1991). *Stress, coping and physical and mental health in two cultures: Taiwan and the United States.* Unpublished doctoral dissertation, Kent State University.

217

Nagin, D. S., & Paternoster, R. (1991). On the relationship of past to future participation in delinquency. *Criminology, 29,* 163-189.

Nakagawa, S., & Cuthill, I. C. (2007). Effect size, confidence interval and statistical significance: A practical guide for biologists. *Biological Review, 82,*591-605.

Nation Police Agent, Ministry of the Interior. (2002). 2000 年世界各國刑案統計比較提要分析。 [2000 worldwide criminal cases comparison and analysis]. Available at http://www.npa.gov.tw/NPAGip/wSite/ct?xItem=26978&ctNode=11398&mp=1

_____ (2009).刑事案件處理嫌疑犯人數－年齡別 。[Criminal cases and suspects-age distribution]. Available at http://www.npa.gov.tw/NPAGip/wSite/lp?ctNode=11395&CtUnit=1740&BaseDSD=7&mp=1

Nation Youth Commission, Executive Yuan. (2005). 青少年政策白皮書。 [Youth policy]. Available at http://www.nyc.gov.tw/

Offer, D., Ostrov, E., Howard, K. I., & Atkinson, R. (1988). The teenage world: Adolescent's self-image in 10 countries. New York, NY: Plenum Medical.

Oishi, S. (2003). Goals as cornerstones of subjective well-being: Linking individuals and cultures. In E. Diener & E. M. Smith (Eds.), *Culture and subjective well-being* (pp.87-112). Cambridge, MA: M.I.T. Press.

Olweus D. (1994). Bullying problems among school children: Long-term outcomes for the victims and an effective school-based intervention program. In L. R. Huesmann (Ed.), *Aggressive behavior: Current perspectives* (pp.411-448). Mahwah, NJ: Lawrence Erlbaum.

Ostrowsky, M. K., & Messner, S. F. (2005). Explaining crime for a young adult population: An application of general strain theory. *Journal of Criminal Justice, 463-476.*

Oyserman, D., Coon, H. M., & Kemmelmeier, M. (2002). Rethinking individualism and collectivism: Evaluation of theoretical assumptions and meta-analyses. *Psychological Bulletin, 128,* 3-72.

Parsons, T. (1951). The social system. Golencoe, IL: Free Press.

Paternoster, R., & Bachman, R. (2001). *Explaining criminals and crime: Essays in contemporary criminological theory.* Los Angeles, CA: Roxbury.

Paternoster, R., Brame, R., Mazerolle, P., & Piquero, A. (1998). Using the correct statistical test for the equality of regression coefficients. *Criminology, 36,* 859-866.

Paternoster, R., & Mazerolle, P. (1994). General strain theory and delinquency: A replication and extension. *Journal of Research in Crime and Delinquency, 31,* 235-263.

Pearlin, L. I. (1989). The sociological study of stress. *Journal of Health and Social Behavior, 30,* 241-256.

Pedhazur, E. J., & Schmelkin, L. P. (1991). *Measurement, design, and analysis: An integrated approach.* Hillsdale, NJ: Lawrence Erlbaum.

Peng, Y. F. (2002). 緊張、負面情緒與青少年偏差行為之研究-以台南地區為例。[A study on strain, negative emotions and juvenile delinquency: A case of Tainan area]. Unpublished master thesis, National Cheng Kung University.

Perez, D. M., Jennings, W. G., & Gover, A. R. (2008). Specifying general strain theory: An ethnically relevant approach. *Deviant Behavior, 29,* 544-578.

Petersen, A. C., Kennedy, R. E., & Sullivan, P. (1991). Coping with adolescence. In M. E. Colton & S. Gore (Eds.), *Adolescent stress: Causes and consequences* (pp.21-42). New York, NY: Aldine de Gruyter.

Piquero, A., Macintosh, R., & Hickman, M. (2002). A validity of a self-reported delinquency scale. *Sociological Methods & Research, 30,* 492-529.

Piquero, N. L., & Sealock, M. D. (2000). Gender and general strain theory: A preliminary test of Broidy and Agnew's gender/GST hypotheses. *Justice Quarterly, 21,* 125-158.

_____ (2004). Gender and general strain theory: A preliminary test of Broidy and Agnew's gender/GST hypotheses. *Justice Quarterly, 21,* 125-158.

Plutchik, R. (1980). *Emotion: A psychoevolutionary synthesis.* New York, NY: Harper & Row.

Pridemore, W. A., Chamlin, M. B., & Cochran, J. K. (2007). An interrupted time-series analysis of Durkheim's social deregulation thesis: The case of the Russian federation. *Justice Quarterly, 24,* 271-290.

Quicker, J. C. (1974). The effect of goal discrepancy on delinquency. *Social Problem, 22,* 76-86.

Radloff, L. S. (1977). A self-report depression scale for research in the general population. *Applied Psychological Measurement, 1,* 385-401.

Raykov, T., & Marcoulides, G. A. (2000). *A first course in structural equation modeling.* Mahwah, NJ: Lawrence Erlbaum.

Research, Development, and Evaluation Commission, Executive Yuan. (2001). 民眾對目前生活及社會問題的看法。[Public opinion on current life situation and social problem]. Available at http://www.rdec.gov.tw/ct.asp?xItem=4023323&ctNode=12142&mp=100

Robbers, M. L. P. (2004). Revisiting the moderating effect of social support on strain: A gendered test. *Sociological Inquiry, 74,* 546-569.

Robinson, D. H., & Levin, J. R. (1997). Reflections on statistical and substantive significance, with a slice of replication. *Educational Research, 26,* 21-26.

Rubin, D. B. (1987). *Multiple imputation for nonresponse in surveys.* New York, NY: Wiley.

_____ (1996). Multiple imputation after 18+ years. *Journal of the American Statitsical Association, 91,* 473-489.

Rubin, D. B., & Schenker, N. (1986). Multiple imputation for interval estimation from simple random samples with ignorable nonresponse. *Journal of the American Statistical Association, 81,* 366-374.

Russell, J. A., & Yik, M. S. M. (1996). Emotions among the Chinese. In M. H. Bond (Ed.), *The handbook of Chinese psychology* (pp.166-188). New York, NY: Oxford University Press.

Sampson, R. J., & Laub, J. H. (1993). *Crime in the making: Pathways and Turning Points through Life.* Cambridge, MA: Harvard University Press.

Sanchez, J. I., Spector, P. E., & Copper, C. L. (2005). Frequently ignored methodological issues in cross-cultural stress research. In P. T. P. Wang & L. C. J. Wong (Eds.), *Handbook of Multicultural Perspectives on Stress and Coping* (pp.29-53). Springer.

Schafer, J. L. (1997). *Analysis of incomplete multivariate data.* London: Chapman & Hall.

Schafer, J. L., & Graham, J. W. (2002). Missing data: Our view of the state of the art. *Psychological Methods, 7,*147-177.

Schafer, J. L., & Olsen M. K. (1998). Multiple imputation for multivariate missing-data problems: A data analyst's perspective. *Multivariate Behavioral Research, 33,* 545-571.

Schneiders, J., Nicolson, N. A., Berkhof, J., Feron, F. J., deVries, M. W., & Os, J. V. (2007). Mood in daily contexts: Relationship with risk in early adolescence. *Journal of Research on Adolescence, 17,* 697-722.

Schreck, C. J. (1999). Victimization and low self-control: An extension and test of a general theory of crime. *Journal of Quantitative Criminology, 16,* 633-654.

Schreck, C. J., Stewart, E. A., & Fisher, B. S. (2006). Self-control, victimization, and their influence on risky lifestyle: A longitudinal analysis using panel data. *Journal of Quantitative Criminology, 22,* 319-340.

Schwartz, S. H. (1990). Individualism-collectivism critique and proposed refinements.

Seiffge-Krenke, I. (2000). Causal links between stressful events, coping style, and adolescent symptomatology. *Journal of Adolescence*, *22,* 675-691.

Selya, R. M. (1995). *Taipei.* New York, NY: John Wiley & Sons.

Sharp, S. F., Brewster, D., & Love, S. R. (2005). Disentangling strain, personal attributes, affective response and deviance: A gendered analysis. *Deviant Behavior, 26,* 133-157.

Sharp, S. F., Terling-Watt, T. T., Atkins, L. A., Gilliam, J. T., & Sanders, A. (2001). Purging behavior in a sample of college females: A research note on general strain theory and female deviance. *Deviant Behavior, 22,* 171-188.

Shaver, P., Schwartz, J., Kirson, D., & O'Connor, C. (1987). Emotion knowledge: Further exploration of a prototype approach. *Journal of Personality of Social Psychology, 52,* 1061-1086.

Shek, D. T. L., & Lee, T. Y. (2007). Parental control and Chinese adolescents in the context of positive youth development programs in Hong Kong. In J. Merrick & A. Omar (Eds.), *Adolescent behavior research: International perspectives* (pp.3-17). New York, NY: Nova Science.

Shi, Y. W. (2004). 國中生生活壓力、負向情緒調適、社會支持與憂鬱情緒之關聯。[The relationships among life stress of junior high school students, negative mood regulation, social support, and depressive mood]. Unpublished master thesis, National Cheng Kung University.

Short, J. F., & Hughes, L. A. (2008). *Juvenile delinquency and delinquents: The nexus of social change.* New Jersey: Pearson Education LTD.

Sigfusdottir, I.-D., Farkas, G., & Silver, E. (2004). The role of depressed mood and anger in the relationship between family conflict and delinquent behavior. *Journal of Youth and Adolescence, 33,* 509-522.

Simons, R. L., & Chen, Y. F., Stewart, E. A., & Brody, G. H. (2003). Incidents of discrimination and risk for delinquency: A longitudinal test of strain theory with an African American sample. *Justice Quarterly, 20,* 827-854.

Sinharay, S., Stern, H. S., & Russell, D. (2001). The use of multiple imputation for the analysis of missing data. *Psychological Methods, 6,* 317-329.

Slocum, L. A., Simpson, S. S., & Smith, D. A. (2005). Strained lives and crime: Examining intra-individual variation in strain and offending in a sample of incarcerated women. *Criminology, 43,* 1067-1110.

Smith, C. S., & Hung, L-C. (2005). *Juvenile delinquency in Taiwan: Sign of times?* Paper presented at the annual meeting of American Society of Criminology, Toronto, Canada.

Sobel, M. E. (1982). Asymptotic confidence intervals for indirect effects in structural equation models. *Sociological Methodology, 13,* 290-312.

Sollenberger, R. T. (1968). Chinese-American child-rearing practices and juvenile delinquency. *Journal of Social Psychology, 74,* 13-23.

Solomon, R. C. (1976). *The passions.* Garden City, NY: Doubleday.

Spielberger, C. D. (1988). *Manual for the sate-trait anger expression inventory* (Research edition). Odessa, FL: Psychological Assessment Resource Inc.

Stafford, M. C. (2004). Juvenile delinquency. In G. Ritzer (Eds.), *Handbook of social problems: A comparative international perspective* (pp.480-494). Thousand Oaks, CA: Sage.

Steinberg, L., & Cauffman, E. (1996). Maturity of judgment in adolescence: Psychosocial factors in adolescent decision making. *Law and Human Behavior, 20,* 249-272.

Steinberg, L., Dornbush, S., & Brown, B. B. (1993). Ethnic differences in adolescent achievement: An ecological perspective. *American Psychologist, 47,* 723-729.

Storch, E. A., Roberti, J. W., & Roth, D. A. (2004). Factor structure, concurrent validity, and internal consistency of the Beck Depression Inventory Second-Edition in a sample of college students. *Depression and Anxiety, 19,* 187-189.

Tanzer, N. K., Sim, C. Q. E., & Speilberger, C. D. (1996). Experience, expression, and control of anger in a Chinese society: The case of Singapore. *Stress and Emotion: Anxiety, Anger, and Curiosity, 16,* 51-65.

Terrell, F., Miller, A. R., Foster, K., & Watkins, C. E. Jr. (2006). Racial discrimination-induced anger and alcohol use among black adolescents. *Adolescence, 41,* 485-492.

Thoits, P. (1983). Dimensions of life events that influence psychological distress: An evaluation and synthesis of the literature. In H. B. Kaplan (Eds.), *Psychological stress: Trends in theory and research* (pp.33-101). New York: Academic Press.

_____ (1995). Stress, coping, and social support process: Where are we? What next? *Journal of Health and Social Behavior, Extra Issue,* 53-79.

Thompson, B. (1993). AERA editorial policies regarding statistical significance testing: Three suggested reform. *Education Research, 25,* 26-30.

Tolan, P. H., & Thomas, P. (1995). The implications of age of onset for delinquency risk II: Logitudinal evidence. *Journal of Abnormal Child Psychology, 23,* 157-182.

Tosun Non-profit Organization. (2001). E 世代青少年網咖經驗調查報告。 [The report of E generation adolescent cyber café experience]. Available at http://www.tosun.org.tw/database_detail.asp?main_id=00002

Tsai, M. H. (2005). 生活壓力、制握信念、社會支持與青少年偏差行為之關係。 [The relationships among life stress, locus of control, social support, and juvenile delinquency]. Unpublished master thesis, National Cheng Kung University.

Trandis, H. C. (1989). The self and social behavior in differing cultural contexts. *Psychological View, 96,* 506-520.

_____ (1994). *Culture and social behavior.* New York, NY: McGraw-Hill.

_____ (1995). *Individualism & Collectivism.* Bulder: Westview Press.

Trojanowicz, R.C., Morash, M., & Schram, P. J. (2001). *Juvenile delinquency: Concepts and control* (6th ed.). NJ: Prentice Hall.

Tung, Y. Y. (2003). 一般化緊張理論的實證性檢驗。 [An empirical test of general strain theory]. 犯罪學期刊, 6, 103-128.

_____ (2007). 社會支持對生活壓迫性因素與年暴力行為間的關聯之影響。 [The effects of social support on strain-juvenile violence relationship]. *Criminal Justice Policy & Crime Research, 10*, 229-247.

Tung, Y. Y., & Wu, Y. L. (2008). 青少年生活緊張與自我傷害之探討。[Discussion on the relationship among juvenile life strain and self-mutilation]. Available at http://www.moj.gov.tw/ct.asp?xItem=98681&ctNode=28261&mp=001

Turner, R. J., & Wheaton, B. (1995). Checklist measurement of Stressful life event. In S. Cohen, R. C. Kessler, & L. U. Gordon (Eds.), *Measuring stress: A guide for health and social scientists* (pp.29-58). New York: Oxford University Press.

Turner, R. J., Wheaton, B., & Lloyd, D. (1995). The epidemiology of social stress. *American Sociological Review, 60*, 104-125.

U.S. Census Bureau. (1990). *United States census 1990* [Data file]. Washington, DC: Available at http://www.census.gov

_____ (2000). *United States census 2000* [Data file]. Washington, DC: Available at http://www.census.gov

_____ (2011). Statistic Abstract. Available at http://www.census.gov/compendia/statab/cats/income_expenditures_poverty_we alth.html

Van de Vijver, F., & Leung, K. (1997). *Methods and data analysis for cross-cultural research.* Thousand Oaks, CA: Sage.

Van Gundy, K. (2002). Gender, the assertion of autonomy, and the stress process in young adulthood. *Social Psychology Quarterly, 65*, 346-363.

Vaux, A., & Ruggiero, M. (1983). Stressful life change and delinquent behavior. *American Journal of Community Psychology, 11*, 169-183.

Verbeke, G., & Molenberghs, G. (2000). *Linear mixed models for longitudinal data.* New York, NY: Springer-Verlag.

Verrill, S. W. (2008). *Social Structure and Social Learning: Mediating or moderating?* El Paso, TX: LFB Scholarly.

Wan, Z. Z. (2001). 台北縣國中生之壓力源、因應方式與生活適應之先關研究。[A study on Taipei county junior high school students' stresses and their coping behaviors]. *生活科學學報, 7,* 61-86.

Wareham, J., Cochran, J. K., Dembo, R., & Sellers, C. S. (2005). Community, strain, and delinquency: A test of a multi-level model of general strain theory. *Western Criminological Review, 6,* 117-133.

Walls, M. L., Chapple, C. L., & Johnson, K. D. (2007). Strain, emotion, and suicide among American Indian youth. *Deviant Behavior, 28,* 219-246.

Wilson, R. W. (1970). *Learning to be Chinese: The political socialization of children n Taiwan.* Cambridge, MA: M.I.T. Press.

Wu, C. (2001). 青少年網路應用問題之探討。 [Discussion on the problem of juvenile internet use]. *Criminal Justice Policy & Crime Research, 4,* 127-140.

Wu, D. Y. H. (1996). Chinese childhood socialization. In M. H. Bond (Ed.), *The handbook of Chinese psychology* (pp.143-154). New York, NY: Oxford University Press.

Xie, H., Farmer, T. W., & Cairns, B. D. (2003). Different forms of aggression among inner-city African-American children: Gender, configurations, and school social network. *Journal of School Psychology, 41,* 355-375.

Xu, C. J., & Xu, C. Z. (2000). 青少年不良幫派成行過程及相關因素之研究。 [A study on the correlates of juvenile gang emerging]. *Criminal Justice Policy & Crime Research, 3,* 77-111.

Xie, J. Q. (1998) 少年飆車行為之分析與防制。 [Analysis and prevention of juvenile joyriding]. *Criminal Justice Policy & Crime Research, 1,* 185-216.

Xu, F. S. (2005). 台灣地區少年非行狀況與防制策略之探討。 [Discussion on Taiwan's juvenile delinquent situation and prevention strategies]. *Criminal Justice Policy & Crime Research, 8,* 265-288.

_____ (2007). 校園暴行之成因與防制策略。 [The causes of school violence and its prevention strategies]. Available at http://www.tosun.org.tw/database_detail.asp?main_id=00038

Xu, F. S., & Hwang, F. M. (2004). 青少年痛苦指數與偏差行為之研究。[Empirical study on the relationship between juvenile negative life index and delinquency]. *Criminal Justice Policy & Crime Research, 7,* 133-158.

Xu, Z. Y. (2005). 緊張因素、負面情緒、制握信念與男女性青少年偏差行為之關聯性研究。[The relationships among strain factors, negative emotions, locus of control and adolescent deviance]. Unpublished master thesis, National Cheng Kung University.

Yamaguchi, S., Kuhlman, D. M., & Sugimori, S. (1995). Personality correlates of allocentric tendencies in individualist and collectivist cultures. *Journal of Cross-Cultural Psychology, 25,* 146-158.

Yang, J. (2004). Taiwan. In M. P. Duffy & S. E. Gillig (Eds.), *Teen gangs: A global view* (pp.179-193). Westport, CT: Greenwood Press.

Yang, K. S. (1986). Chinese personality and its change. In M. H. Bond (Ed), *The Psychology of the Chinese People* (pp.107-170). New York, NY: Oxford University Press.

_____ (1995). Chinese social orientation: An integrative analysis. In T. Y. Lin, W. S. Tseng, & E. K. Yeh (Eds.), *Chinese societies and mental health* (pp.19-39). New York, NY: Oxford University Press.

Yang, K. S., & Lu, L. (2005). Social- and individual-oriented self-actualizer: Conceptual analysis and empirical assessment of their psychological characteristics. *Indigenous Psychological Research in Chinese Societies, 23,* 71-143.

Yi, C. C., & Wu, C. L. (2004). Taiwan. In J. J. Slater (Ed.), *Teen life in Asia* (pp.223-241). Westport, CT: Greenwood Press.

Yoshihama, M. (2002). Battered women's coping strategies and psychological distress: Differences by immigration status. *American Journal of Community Psychology, 30,* 429-452.

Yu, A. B. (1996). Ultimate life concerns, self, and Chinese achievement motivation. In M. H. Bond (Ed.), *The handbook of Chinese psychology* (pp.227-246). New York, NY: Oxford University Press.

Zeng, H. Q. (2008). 青少年藥物濫用問題分析。[Analysis of juvenile drug abuse problem] (National Policy Foundation, Culture and Education Analysis 097-011). Available at http://www.npf.org.tw/post/3/4293

Zhang, W. B. (2003). *Taiwan's modernization: Americanization, modernizing Confucian manifestations.* River Edge, NJ: World Scientific.

Zhou, B. S. (2000). 台灣地區在校青少年藥物使用流行病學調查研究。[Epidemiological study on illicit drug abuse by school adolescents in Taiwan]. Taipei, Taiwan: Department of Health, Executive Yuan, Taiwan.

Zhou, S. X. (2001). 愛上學的孩子，不會變壞嗎？論學校因素與青少年偏差行為之關係。[Children who love to go to school will not be bad? The relationship between school factors and juvenile delinquency]. *應用心理學研究, 11,* 93-115.

APPENDICES

Appendix A: Survey questionnaire

Delinquency (both U.S. and Taiwan version)
Have you ever…in the past 12 months?
1. Purposely damaged or destroyed property that did not belong to you.
2. Hit someone with the idea of hurting them.
3. Used alcohol.
   Response: 0 = No, never; 1 = Yes
Aggression (both U.S. and Taiwan version)
How many times in the past 12 months have you…?
1. Used physical actions (such as slapping, kicking, or hitting hard) against a brother or sister.

Response: 1 = Never; 2 = Once; 3 = Twice; 4 = 3-5times; 5 = 6 or more times;
        6 = no brother/sister
Goal strain scale (both U.S. and Taiwan version)
How much do you agree or disagree with the following statements?
1. The teachers here embarrass you when you don't know the right answers (respect).
2. My teachers don't respect my opinions as much as I would like (respect).
3. My parents don't respect my opinions as much as I would like (respect).
4. My classmates do not like me (relationship with others).
5. People my age tend to push me around (relationship with others).
6. My parents don't give me a say in what the rules should be (autonomy).
7. People my age treat me like I'm still a kid (autonomy).
Response: 1 = Strongly agree; 2 = Agree; 3 = Disagree; 4 = Strongly disagree

Unjust strain scale (both U.S. and Taiwan version)
How much do you agree or disagree with the following statements?
1. Many students don't study as hard as I do, but they still make better grades.
2. I don't have as much money as other students in this school.
3. Even though I try hard, my grades are never good enough.
4. Other students get special favors from the teachers here that I don't get.
5. Even though I work hard, I never seem to have enough money.
6. Compared to the rules my friends have to abide by, the rules my parents set for me are unfairly strict.
7. No matter how responsible I try to be, my parents don't trust me to do things on my own.
Response: 1 = Strongly agree; 2 = Agree; 3 = Disagree; 4 = Strongly disagree
Negative Life-event scale (both U.S. and Taiwan version)
Which of the following things happened to you in the past 12 months?
1. Change schools.
2. Parents divorced .
3. Parent moved out or away.
4. Broke up with boyfriend or girlfriend.

229

5. Moved to new neighborhood.
6. Death of a relative.
7. Lost a friendship.
8. Pet died or disappeared.
9. Dropped from or quit athletic team or school activities.
10. Parents lost job for more than two months.
Response: 0 = No; 1 = Yes

Victimization scale (both U.S. and Taiwan version)
Have the following things ever been done to you personally?
1. Been picked on or teased by other kids who were being mean.
2. Had your backpack, lunch money, or other personal things stolen from you.
3. Had a bicycle or motorcycle stolen.
4. Been hit by someone trying to hurt you.
5. Had someone use a weapon or force to get money or things from you.
6. Been attacked by someone with a weapon or by someone trying to serious hurt or kill you.
Response: 0 = No; 1 = Yes

Anger scale (both U.S. and Taiwan version)
How often do you think these statements describe you?
1. I feel annoyed when people don't notice that I've done good work.
2. When I get mad, I say nasty things.
3. It makes me very mad when I am criticized in front of others.
4. When I get frustrated, I feel like hitting others.
5. I feel furious when I work hard but get a poor grade.
6. It makes me mad that others are able to spend more money than I can.
7. It makes me mad when I don't get the respect from others that I deserve.
8. If things upset other people, it's their problem, not mine.
Response: 1 = Almost never; 2 =Sometimes; 3 = Often; 4 = Almost always

Depression scale (both U.S. and Taiwan version)
How often do you think these statements describe you?
1. I find it hard to keep my mind on school work.
2. I don't look forward to things as much as I used to.
3. I sleep very well.
4. I have lots of energy.
Response: 1 = Almost never; 2 =Sometimes; 3 = Often; 4 = Almost always

Appendix B: EFA tables

Table B1 Principal Axis Factor Analysis for Goal Strain and Unjust Strain

Factor	Factor Loadings	
	U.S.	Taiwan
Goal strain		
Goal strain1-teacher does not respect me	.452	.669
Goal strain2-parents do not respect me	.623	.725
Goal strain3-teachers embarrass you	.422	.569
Goal strain4-parents do not give me a say	.533	.686
Goal strain5-people treat me like a kid	.576	.503
Goal strain6-my classmates do not like me*	.443	.530
Goal strain7-people push me around	.441	.537
Sum of squared loadings	1.775	2.591
Unjust strain		
Unjust strain1-students do not study hard but make better grade	.323	.318
Unjust strain2-I do not have as much money as other students	.361	.452
Unjust strain3-my grades are never good enough even I try hard	.539	.423
Unjust strain4-other students get special favors from teachers	.365	.443
Unjust strain5-I never seem to have enough money	.585	.596
Unjust strain6-my parents set unfairly strict rules	.496	.550
Unjust strain7-my parents do not trust me to do things on my own	.532	.623
Sum of square loadings	1.529	1.726

*Reverse coded

231

Table B2 Principal Axis Factor Analysis for Anger and Depression

Factor	Factor Loadings	
	U.S.	Taiwan
Anger		
Anger1-I feel annoyed if people do not notice my good work	.507	.550
Anger2-when I get mad, I say nasty things	.485	.509
Anger3-I get very mad when I am criticized in front of others	.616	.671
Anger4-When I get frustrated, I feel like hitting something	.470	.607
Anger5-I feel furious when I work hard but get a poor grade	.557	.517
Anger6-I feel mad when people do not let me make my	.555	.642
Anger7-I feel mad that others have more money than I do	.539	.461
Anger8-I feel mad when I do not get respect that I deserve	.614	.624
Sum of squared loadings	2.378	2.661
Depression		
Depression1-I find it hard to keep my mind on school work	.349	.106
Depression2-I do not look forward to things	.475	.149
Depression3-I sleep very well*	.575	.793
Depression4-I have lots of energy*	.484	.784
Sum of square loadings	.913	1.277

*Reverse coded

CPSIA information can be obtained at www.ICGtesting.com
Printed in the USA
LVOW07s1120120715

445928LV00002BA/451/P